Inspiring, educational, and relevant, *Wild Success* is a brilliant combination of living at the edge of human performance, real-world application, and fascinating insights into our mind. It's both personal and ubiquitous in its narrative. From the start of each chapter, the stories of adventure and perseverance draw you in and then subtly shift to issues that impact us all . . . purpose, adversity, resilience, risk, balance. Amy and Kevin have managed to craft the CliffsNotes version of how to live a successful and fulfilling life. This is a not a book that you read once, but one that you refer to . . . continuously.
— Shawn Seamans, President, McKesson Life Sciences

This book is a must-read for anyone who wants to get ahead in business! It kept me captivated from end to end. Being both an adventurer and an entrepreneur I found it especially captivating and useful. There are some excellent lessons that I will be applying to my own business strategies as we continue growing our own company.
— Colin Angus, National Geographic Adventurer of the Year who completed the first human-powered journey around the world

These stories of adventure, grounded with respected academic and scientific research, provide inspiration and guidance to those interested in enhancing their understanding and practice of leadership. It is a valuable reminder of the lessons we can take from individuals who encourage us to question our own limitations and reach our fullest potential and possibilities.
— Robert N. Thomas, PhD, Professor of Leadership, Institute of Leadership and Entrepreneurship, Scheller College of Business, Georgia Institute of Technology

The business world is ruthless to those who are not prepared to handle its ever-changing tides. Amy Posey and Kevin Vallely have marvelously connected the important lessons from adventuring in the great wilderness to achieving success and becoming a solid business leader. It will open your mind and push you to think of how you can take control of yourself and learn a delicate discipline in pushing toward success. What can save your life in the world of adventure can propel you to greatness in business.
— Manal AlBayat, Chief Community Engagement Officer, Expo 2020 Dubai

What a brilliant move to embed business and management principles into extreme adventure stories, making it more likely to remember them. Enduring principles emerge when humans are severely tested.

—Sam Sullivan, Canadian politician, current MLA
for Vancouver-False Creek, 38th mayor
of Vancouver, British Columbia

The connections between the adventure world and the business world are clear, concise, and plain to see. An adventurer's experience can help instruct every leader to perform at their best.

—Sir Ranulph Fiennes, described by the *Guinness Book of
World Records* as "the world's greatest living explorer"

A beautiful piece of work that allows each of us to see how to leverage our own vulnerabilities and shortcomings to transform our leadership potential. *Wild Success* somehow manages to strike that delicate balance of being both intellectually and practically compelling—and you come out inspired to venture into unchartered territory to up your leadership game.

—Sarah Gretczko, Chief Learning and Skills Officer, Mastercard

Wild Success is an adventure book, a personal development book, and a life and business manual. Follow these outstanding real-life adventurers as they row the Atlantic and the Pacific Oceans, summit Everest, undertake polar exploration, circumnavigate Antarctica, and even pioneer personal jet-propelled flight. Learn how they apply lessons in neuroscience, growth mindset, and perseverance to survive and how you can apply these lessons and achieve your *Wild Success* in business and life.

—Richard Bailey, President and Chief
Transformation Officer, HP Inc.

Whether on the water, in the forest, crossing the tundra, or climbing to the summit, wild nature is good for our bodies and minds. Posey, Vallely, and a team of adventurous souls expertly guide leaders and readers into the heart of their own wild creativity, focused purpose, and peak performance in life, work, and play. This is extreme sports made powerfully practical.

—Dr. Wallace J Nichols, author of the
New York Times bestseller *Blue Mind*

Wild Success has a fresh perspective on achieving peak performance. It weaves the principles of success in adventuring together with practical outcomes in the business world, drawing on parallels that make for refreshing reading and insights.

—Arthur Hu, Chief Information Officer, Lenovo

Looking for an edge? Read *Wild Success* cover to cover. Twice. Why? Because Kevin and Amy have codified what it takes to excel at the edge of human capacity. Fascinating, accessible, and just plain fun, this book will be your guide as you embark on your next audacious business (ad)venture.

—Dr. Greg Wells, PhD, Performance Physiologist,
www.drgregwells.com

It is not often that you get your hands on a life-transforming book, one that somehow manages to be at once inspiring, exhilarating, and educational, but *Wild Success*, by Kevin Vallely and Amy Posey, is one of them. Taking readers to the most extreme places, the book gives deeply personal accounts of how great adventurers overcome monumental challenges; but then, using brilliant analysis and research, it goes further, letting us all understand the deep dynamic of resilience and creativity. Leadership books are all too often vanity exercises of one-dimensional, successful people, but the stories in *Wild Success* are forged by courageous people in the most unforgiving places, places where vanity means death. The courage to overcome obstacles is not abstract in these accounts, but all too real and hard-earned, and the lessons learned offer an invaluable resource for anyone who wants to truly succeed in business and, more importantly, in the adventure of life. *Wild Success* is a unique, brilliant, thrilling, thoughtful book that is a must-read for any aspiring leader and anyone who dreams of living their best life.

—Evan Solomon, the new host of CTV News Channel's
"Power Play," a Canadian political journalist, radio
host, and writer for *Maclean's* magazine

Our individual lives are like "endurance" expeditions, filled with twists and turns, successes and failures, awe and wonder, and constant decisions and choices. *Wild Success* delivers inspirational nuggets that we can all use to reflect, dream big, embrace flexibility, find passion and purpose, and fine tune our skills to be better leaders of our own life-journeys.

—Geoff Green, C.M., C.Q., FRCGS, FI'03, PhD (Hons),
Founder and President, Students on Ice Foundation

WILD
SUCCESS

WILD
SUCCESS

7 Key Lessons Business Leaders Can Learn from Extreme Adventurers

AMY POSEY and **KEVIN VALLELY**

New York Chicago San Francisco Athens London Madrid
Mexico City Milan New Delhi Singapore Sydney Toronto

1 2 3 4 5 6 7 8 9   LCR   25 24 23 22 21 20

ISBN   978-1-260-45551-9
MHID   1-260-45551-3

e-ISBN   978-1-260-45552-6
e-MHID   1-260-45552-1

McGraw-Hill Education books are available at special quantity discounts to use as premiums and sales promotions or for use in corporate training programs. To contact a representative, please visit the Contact Us pages at www.mhprofessional.com.

Contents

Introduction   vii

CHAPTER 1   *Cognitive Reappraisal: A Different Perspective*   1

CHAPTER 2   *Grit: The Passion to Prevail*   25

CHAPTER 3   *Growth Mindset: Sitting Still Means Going Backward*   53

CHAPTER 4   *Purpose: Finding Your Spark*   77

CHAPTER 5   *Innovation: Big Dreams and Big Struggles*   103

CHAPTER 6   *Resilience: Bouncing Forward*   127

CHAPTER 7   *Personal Sustainability: Building Balance*   157

Conclusion   185

Notes   193

Additional Resources   203

Acknowledgments   205

Index   209

Introduction

dventurers are the paragons of human performance. They push the limits of perceived human ability, muster the courage to test themselves, and forge unknown paths to discover what's truly possible. Their stories from the wildest, most testing environments on the planet let us garner unique insights. We learn how to perform at our best, despite the most demanding of circumstances. These remarkable women and men implicitly understand what it means to execute under pressure, because their very existence often depends on it. *Wild Success* introduces you to some of these special individuals and lets you join them in their rarified world of high adventure to catch a glimpse of what makes them tick. In their stories, you will discover what drives them to the highest levels of performance and you will come to understand the "special something," those qualities of performance that we can all tap into to be better.

Wild Success is a book about leadership. In it, you will discover how the leadership lessons learned in the extreme adventure world connect directly to today's business environment and our day-to-day work. Authors Amy Posey and Kevin Vallely will take you on an exciting journey into the world of these extreme adventurers and explain how the insights from a surfer atop a monstrous 50-foot wave or a resilient yet exhausted polar skier clawing across the Antarctic plateau can help you, as a leader, perform at your best. Combining hard-won lessons from the adventure world with innovative research and stories from the fields of neuroscience and business, the authors will explain how the "wild wisdom" garnered by elite adventurers in the most extreme environments on the planet is just as valuable in the modern-day workplace.

* * *

We, the authors, are Amy Posey and Kevin Vallely. We are writers, adventurers, and business professionals. Throughout *Wild Success*, we will use the pronoun *we*, rather than *I*, because this book was a true team effort. Both of us have been involved in every aspect of its crafting and feel that our collective voice tells a more complete story. The only place we will take the liberty of referencing each other in the singular is when we describe each other and explain why we are individually qualified to speak more specifically to a story or lesson shared.

Most of the adventurers profiled in *Wild Success* have been connected together by an individual named Shane Toohey, who has a particular gift for identifying exceptional people and integrating them into his leadership development consulting firm—The AIP Group. His ability to identify talent and connect people made this book a reality. The *AIP* in the company's name is an acronym that stands for "Adventures Inspiring Performance" and defines at its core what the company does and what this book is about. Amy and Kevin both work as facilitators with The AIP Group and, thanks to this connection, have been able to come together to write this book. Both Amy and Kevin bring a unique set of insights and skills to the writing, making for a compelling and educational read that is grounded in research and science.

Amy Posey has spent the last 20 years as a management consultant and leadership expert, and, prior to working with The AIP Group, spent 10 years at Deloitte, delivering internal leadership development programs as well as learning, change, and communication solutions to global technology companies. She has focused her work on driving high performance in individuals and teams and decided to increase her capabilities by adding neuroscience research to her work. Amy earned her Executive Master's with distinction in applied neuroscience and leadership from the Neuroleadership Institute, and combined with her MBA from DePaul University, she has been able to more effectively drive performance by connecting the science of performance to business outcomes. Additionally, she has a BA in English, education, and writing with distinction from Purdue University. Amy is the former CEO of Peak Teams (before it became The AIP Group) and is the founder and current CEO of the neuroscience-based manager development company SUPER*MEGA*BOSS. She is also passionate about adventure herself, having hiked and climbed (and in many cases, paragliding off of) mountains on all seven continents.

Kevin Vallely is both a business professional and world-class explorer, and he fully understands how the wild wisdom garnered in the adventure world correlates to the challenges faced by the modern business professional because he lives it himself. He juggles his life as a registered architect, leadership mentor, author, keynote speaker, and father, yet still has found the time to become an internationally recognized explorer. His adventuring career spans nearly two decades, with one of his many highlights happening in 2009, when he and two teammates broke the world record for the fastest unsupported trek to the geographic

South Pole. Kevin is a member of the esteemed Explorer's Club and was honored as an Explorer's Club Flag recipient for his expedition to the Northwest Passage in 2013. His book on this adventure, *Rowing the Northwest Passage: Adventure, Fear, and Awe in a Rising Sea,* was published in 2017.

We had talked about writing *Wild Success* many, many times, but as adventurers ourselves, the exciting opportunities of the expedition world always drew us out before we could sit down and put pen to paper. Not too long ago, the two of us spent six months planning for and embarking on an expedition together, as part of a large 11-person team, crossing Baffin Island in the Canadian High Arctic, the fifth-largest island in the world, in winter, on foot in 2018. We examined what a high-performing team could do in an unforgiving and ever-changing environment, as our own study in human and team performance, and realized that we had to write this book. So over the last year, we have done exactly that. We have paused and studied the modern-day adventurer to learn how he or she has accomplished the seemingly impossible and how their experience can inform our performance as well, in the business world and beyond.

Our position in writing this book is unique as we are both adventurers and leadership development facilitators. We not only have heard stories from the adventure world, but have both immersed ourselves in the challenges and changes happening in the business world. The lessons learned from extreme adventures relate directly to the constantly changing business environment, because we have seen performance on both ends of the spectrum. Working with Fortune 500 companies, small and medium businesses, and startups, we have witnessed teams and organizations learn tough lessons around innovation, we have seen them be resilient in downward-trending markets and drive toward seemingly impossible goals through establishing a sense of purpose and alignment. When provided a different context for thinking about performance—the context of adventure— we have watched people ranging from first-time managers to experienced CEOs gain perspective and insight about their own work performance through the parallel lessons drawn.

The adventurers we have profiled within *Wild Success* are all remarkable individuals who are exemplars of high performance. Their stories are compelling and captivating, where they're often pushing themselves to the extreme or encountering the seemingly impossible. Each chapter of *Wild Success* is a profile of one (and in one case, a pair) of these adventurers and highlights a key capacity, quality, or trait that has been instrumental to their success. We then draw out those fundamental lessons from their experience and provide you with some practical tips and advice so that modern leaders can use these stories and lessons to drive themselves to higher performance.

The Litmus Test of High Performance

In 1913, as the legend goes, an advertisement ran in a London newspaper seeking the following: "MEN WANTED for hazardous journey, small wages, bitter cold, long months of complete darkness, constant danger, safe return doubtful, honour and recognition in case of success."

Can you imagine answering this call by explorer Sir Ernest Shackleton to join his Imperial Trans-Antarctic Expedition? If you can, you get a glimpse into the mind of the adventurer. Over 1,000 people answered this call.[1] For them, this simple message boomed enticing and loud. Its words were a promise of something special, a guarantee of excitement and challenge that would transcend the mundane and thrust them into the unknown. To those people, to those adventurers among us, Shackleton's words were impossible to ignore and were a rally cry to be followed. These are the type of people we have chosen to profile in *Wild Success*. Unafraid of the most dangerous of challenges, excited by the unknown, and optimistic of the future, these are the incredible people we have selected to learn from.

Adventurers are the litmus test for human performance. If they do not perform at their best, they may never do so again. In *Wild Success*, you will discover what makes modern-day adventurers tick. You will learn how they view obstacles and setbacks and think differently about the challenges they face. You will come to understand how they grow their resilience and grit while building an optimistic view of the world around them. And you will discover how these unique individuals defy the odds, innovate on the fly, and courageously excel where most fear to tread. Our aspiration in writing this book is to engage and inspire you with stories from both the adventure and business worlds while providing concrete performance tips, based in current understandings in neuroscience, that will let you grow and thrive as a leader.

We want to thank all the adventurers profiled in *Wild Success* for working with us and sharing their inspiring stories so we can learn from them. Although many of them claim to be ordinary people doing extraordinary things, we think they are all simply extraordinary.

You will meet one of the world's greatest big wave surfers, Mark Mathews, and come to understand how he used the power of cognitive reappraisal to face a life-changing accident that threatened to end his career. You will travel the wild open oceans in a rowboat with Roz Savage, the four-time Guinness World

Record holder in ocean rowing, as she navigates the tumult of life and sea to find her true purpose. North Pole explorer Matt McFadyen will demonstrate the power of a growth mindset as he unshackles himself from meager beginnings to become an internationally recognized explorer and leadership development professional and speaker, only to continue to face challenges in both the adventure and business worlds. You will come to understand the true meaning of resilience as you join Lisa Blair in her desperate attempt to save herself as she is confronted with a dismasting on the Southern Ocean in the midst of a perilous storm while circumnavigating Antarctica. Paul Gleeson and Tori Holmes will take you on an ocean journey as well, but theirs will demonstrate how the power of grit can help you reach the unlikeliest of goals as pure novices. Mountaineer and wingsuit pilot Rex Pemberton will prove to all why adventurers are innovators, as he evolves from the youngest Australian to climb Mount Everest to become a pioneer in individual human flight. Finally, Kevin Vallely, the coauthor of this book, will share how he uses personal sustainability to maintain a positive balance in his life so he can achieve an astonishing list of accomplishments in adventure, including his own Guinness World Record in polar exploration.

As we mentioned before, most of the adventurers profiled in *Wild Success* have been brought together because of another extraordinary individual, Shane Toohey. Shane's belief, like ours, is that the insight and wisdom garnered in the adventure world has a direct correlation to tumult faced by leaders and people in the corporate experience. His philosophy has always been that by sharing stories from the adventure world and discovering the wild wisdom these stories have to offer, we will be inspired to achieve our own peak capability. He has made a career of bringing this philosophy to life.

Shane's own adventure story is noteworthy in its own right. It was the catalyst for the creation of his company The AIP Group. It all began in 1990s when Shane was a prolific mountaineer and first descent skier, tackling some of the most challenging mountains on the planet. "I had a corporate job as a marketing professional," he says, "but the rest of my time was spent climbing and skiing. It was a juggle, mate, but I made it work." Things came to a head for Shane when he was planning an expedition to Antarctica and he was laid off from his job. At the time, Shane had made first ski-descents on six of the seven continents, with only Antarctica left to ski to make it the continental grand slam. Skiing in Antarctica would be a huge boost to his adventuring career, but now after losing his job, he wondered how feasible it was. "I had enough money to get there," he said, "but it was the money that my wife, Vik, and I had saved up for a down payment on a house in Sydney. Vik knew how important this expedition was to me and in the end, she said, 'Do it. We'll manage OK.' So I did it."

It was pivotal decision for Shane, and ultimately one that would change his life forever. His journey took him by boat from the tip of South America at Cape Horn across the infamous Drake Passage to Antarctica. It was halfway across this section of ocean, considered by many to be among the world's roughest, that Shane's voyage became even tougher. "The head guide knocked on my cabin door and told me I wasn't going to be allowed to ski when we landed," says Shane. "'You're the only skier in our group of clients' he said, 'We don't have enough guides on board to have one accompany you. We can't allow you ski.'"

Shane was stunned. He had sacrificed everything to take this journey and now, of no fault of his own, was told his expedition was over before it started. "I flipped out at first," he said, "but

I contained myself pretty quickly. I was determined to change their minds." Shane paused, crafted his argument, and then sat down with the expedition leaders on the boat and made his case. He soon recognized he was in his element, using his negotiation tactics from business to make his argument, understanding how to parlay his marketing expertise into the most powerful of sales pitches. "I communicated clearly to them why I needed to do this and why they were going to let me do it," he says. Shane detailed his experience as a mountaineer and skier and made the leaders understand he was exceedingly capable in doing what he had set out to do. He rallied their spirit of adventure as well. "I explained to them how this was my final chapter in my bid to ski all seven continents and got them excited and motivated to help me achieve my goal, too."

Shane would ski the steep slopes of the Antarctic continent and fulfill his dream of skiing all seven continents. While standing alone atop Two Hummock Island on the Antarctic Peninsula, preparing to make his final descent, he had an epiphany. He realized now that his leadership instincts were stimulated and empowered in the unpredictable and dynamic environments he faced. He recognized that through his adventures something special was roused in him that would not only let him perform at his peak as a mountaineer and skier but perform at his best in anything that he pursued. The results of those lessons were clear, and he had proved it to himself from the top of that icy, distant mountain peak.

Looking out over the Southern Ocean, as far from the rigors of the daily grind as almost anyone on the planet, Shane reflected about the life he wanted to return to. Was he going to head back to another corporate job and continue juggling his two disparate pursuits, or was there a way for him to integrate his passion for the mountains into something that would help other leaders with big decisions? Maybe he could somehow use adventure as a platform to teach important leadership skills in the corporate world? In that moment and that decision the concept of The AIP Group was born.

It has been nearly 20 years since that day, and The AIP Group has grown into a successful business accruing the wild wisdom garnered in the adventure world and bringing it back to the boardroom. Shane has successfully assembled a team of world-class adventurers over the last two decades who exhibit powerful leadership skills. These adventurers plan and execute expeditions with teams to the extreme parts of the planet that are filmed and crafted into decision-making simulations in these complex, changing environments. The team has undertaken extreme expeditions to every corner of the globe, including climbing Mount Cook, the crown jewel of the New Zealand Alps; summiting Mount Everest, the world's highest peak; kayaking the crocodile-infested waters of the Okavango Delta in Botswana; and surfing the largest waves on the planet, including the infamous Jaws wave in Hawaii. On each expedition, the team tackles extreme challenges, all the while filming, pushing their limits, improving their performance, and creating the stories that inspire people to grow and develop. Both of us have spent the last decade sharing these simulations, stories, and lessons globally, and now we share these lessons with you.

In May 2013, after just completing a daring ski descent down the Grand Teton in Wyoming, Shane traveled to Chamonix, France, to attempt several challenging ski descents in the Alps. He was on the north face of the Aiguille du Midi, on a hanging glacier called Glacier Rond, when something went terribly wrong. He had just skirted left to avoid the 200-foot vertical face of the massive glacier and entered the 2,000-foot couloir when caught an edge of his ski and fell. He doesn't recall anything of the accident, but his two companions witnessed a terrifying, uncontrolled, head-first fall down the ice-covered 2,000-foot face. Miraculously, he survived, but was left badly hurt with a traumatic brain injury.

Shane spent months in a small hospital in France, and over this time, the AIP team would realize the extent of Shane's brain injury. As the charismatic lead facilitator for the company, Shane now struggled with most basic of functions like walking, talking, short-term memory, sleeping, seeing clearly, or even writing his name. The bruises and scrapes on his body healed quickly, but not so his brain. He no longer functioned as he once did, and he could no longer be the face of his own business.

In creating The AIP Group, Shane had brought together a group of exceptional individuals who could successfully navigate the most challenging environments on the planet. In each of these people he saw something special, something truly extraordinary that chartered their success. They, like him, intuitively knew that if you can thrive in the wildly unpredictable world of extreme adventure, you can thrive anywhere you choose. They were motivated by Shane's ideas and inspired by how he led. Now, at his lowest point in his life, they needed to stand behind the leader who had stood behind them for so long and apply those lessons of resilience to step in on his behalf and learn how to drive and grow the business in this new context.

Over the following six years, The AIP Group worked through the complicated nature of running a small business as Shane healed. While Shane made his slow and difficult recovery, the team learned how to work within a new context and paradigm to continue AIP's success. At this writing, thanks to their efforts, The AIP Group continues to grow and share leadership lessons, the most important of which is the lesson Shane himself learned, that surrounding yourself with a team of caring, capable, and resilient people who are aligned toward a common goal can lift you in your hardest moments. Because of this team of adventurers, he is in a better place than he has ever been.

If you aspire to push past self-imposed boundaries and be the best that you can be, then read on. In the coming pages you will be engaged and inspired with stories from both the adventure and business worlds that will let you grow and thrive as a leader. The wisdom garnered by the adventurers we profile maps directly to the challenges you face as a person and a professional. You will find meaningful applications in the research outlined in this book and come away with tactics and tips gleaned from both the adventurers and the business leaders we have profiled that will propel you to your own wild success!

CHAPTER 1

Cognitive Reappraisal

A Different Perspective

I t's October 2016. Mark Mathews is about to surf a terrifying wave on the south coast of New South Wales, Australia, and he's not feeling right. Mark is one of the best big wave surfers in the world and is feeling the pressure to perform. He's only been back surfing for a month now after a nine-month-long recovery from a serious shoulder injury he suffered on the infamous Jaws wave in Maui, and he knows he's pushing his recovery in order to be back. "I was nervous about getting hurt again," he says, "I had never surfed this wave before."[1]

The wave he's preparing to surf is called a slab wave. Until recent years, it was the type of wave considered unrideable by the surf community—a beast simply too fast to surf. A slab wave occurs when a fast-moving swell traversing over deep water abruptly hits a shallow reef and bursts upward. Within seconds a hungry, thick tube of water is born, its open maw racing forward, eagerly sucking up all the water from the shallows in front of it. But as quickly as it rises, the slab wave falls, violently slamming shut, pulverizing everything beneath in it. A surfer riding one of these collapsing monsters is akin to a skier outrunning an avalanche.

Unlike traditional waves that slow down as they grow in height, slab waves lose none of their momentum as they grow, hurtling into shore with the speed and energy of a runaway freight train. For a surfer without propulsion, generating enough momentum to hop aboard one of these speedy monsters was physically impossible until motorized watercraft changed the equation. Using a jet-ski to tow them up to speed, surfers with the requisite skill and courage found themselves able to access the inaccessible and were now able to surf waves they could only dream about before. A new extreme cousin to surfing was born, a discipline as exhilarating as it was deadly.

Mark holds tightly to the towline as he accelerates, the scream of the jet ski in front of him barely audible over the thunder of crashing waves. He's favoring his right arm over his left because of his shoulder injury, but he feels good enough to surf. For the inexperienced surfer, the scene unfolding before Mark would be that of a war zone—the cacophony of heaving swell casting the ocean into wild disarray while the unrelenting concussive thud of waves against reef explode like bombs everywhere. For Mark, the discord of the environment is one that he's learned to understand and even find a rhythm in. Instead of becoming paralyzed with fear, he simply holds the towline a little tighter and looks for his next ride.

Mark Mathews surfing in the thick barrel of a slab wave   *Courtesy of AIP Group, Mark Mathews*

Before Mark surfs a dangerous wave like the one he's facing, he performs a set pre-surf ritual to put his mind into focus. It is something he does every time. "Fear is a big part of what I do," he says, "so dealing with it effectively is critical to my performance." Using simple breathing techniques to slow his mind down, Mark concentrates on feelings of excitement rather than anxiety, while reflecting on why he is doing what he is doing. "I think about my family and friends . . . about my career," he says, "and then I focus on exactly what I'll be doing, focusing on the outcome in the barrel, how good I'm going to feel." Today, Mark has undertaken his pre-surf ritual, but his recent injury has still sowed some doubt.

Mark's jet-ski driver, Tyge Landa, arcs left as Mark feels the building speed of the water beneath him. He lets go of the towline and the ocean tilts forward. He drops down what has quickly become a shear face of water. "There's no feeling like it," he explains, "You get inside the barrel, and for two to three seconds you get to stand back as you're surrounded by the ocean, all the energy, and it's unbelievable! It's the best feeling I've ever felt in my life."[2]

The wave at eight feet is small by Mark's big wave standards, but for what it lacks in height, it makes up for in speed, girth, and unpredictability. It is easily one of the most challenging waves he's ever surfed. Mark's first ride is perfect as he sweeps out the end of the glowing green barrel and rides safely over the remaining lip. Mark's second wave is also in the eight-foot range, but is chunkier than the first. He doesn't like it and attempts to escape. "I tried to dive off early and get out the back of the wave so I wouldn't have to deal with a wipeout. The wave picked me up and slammed me feet first into the reef."[3] The rest becomes a blur.

Mark lies in his hospital bed confused and disoriented. His right leg is surrounded with a steel frame looking like construction scaffolding, as metal rods attached to it puncture through the skin of his leg and anchor it in place. He looks on with a sense of disassociation and disbelief, the leg in front of him could be anyone's—he can't feel a thing.

Mark's right leg took the full impact of the wipeout when he was slammed onto the reef. The force of the blow dislocated his knee, fractured his shin, ruptured his anterior and posterior cruciate ligaments, and ripped through his artery and nerve. He was immediately airlifted to Canberra Hospital, where doctors feared the worst. In an interview with *Stab* magazine's Jed Smith, Mark describes the doctor's initial prognosis. "He was telling my [girlfriend Brittany]—I didn't really know any of this—but [the doctor] walked out of the room and was like, I don't know if I can save it [the leg]," he says. "And Brit was like, 'Nah, you've got the wrong person. My boyfriend is Mark Mathews.'"[4]

Brittany's feeling of disbelief is understandable. Mark Mathews is one of the best big wave surfers on the planet, the winner of an unprecedented three consecutive Oakley Big Wave Awards. He is an icon of his sport, and surfing is his life. As a professional athlete, more than anyone, he can't afford to lose his leg, yet there he was.

By a stroke of luck, one of Australia's best surgeons was on duty at the Canberra Hospital that day and was able to save Mark's leg. "The surgeon came out and said: 'An hour longer and your leg would have had to have been amputated,'" Mark explains. "And I had to wait three days to see what would happen." The surgeon used a section of artery from Mark's upper leg to repair the damage done to his lower, and now he needed to wait to see if it would take hold. "For the next three days it was terrifying. I was looking at my foot the whole time," he says. "Brittany was there with me and she was checking every hour to see if the pulse had come back." On the third day she felt something.

"I was in pain all day, every day in hospital. I tried to practice gratitude," he says with a laugh, shaking his head, "but there wasn't much to be grateful for." Then something unexpected happened.

A young boy on a lower floor of the hospital named Jason came up to visit him. He had been a surfer himself and heard on social media that Mark Mathews, a hero of his, was in the same hospital. He came up to pay a visit and to chat. "He rolled into my room in an electric chair," says Mark, his voice quiet now, "the kid . . . he was just a kid . . . he was in a wheelchair. He was quadriplegic. He broke his neck mountain biking." A switch flipped in Mark. "Straight away, complete change in the way I perceived my situation," says Mark, his voice much more animated now. "Now, all of a sudden, I was the luckiest man on earth that I wasn't in his chair, that poor kid."

Mark would remain in the hospital for the next three months. Surgeons would make two huge incisions on either side of his lower leg to relieve the pressure and would attach vacuum bags on each side to draw out excess fluid. The gaping holes in his lower leg are over a foot long and over two inches wide. To the untrained eye the wounds look like the gruesome output of some low-budget horror movie, and they would remain open like that for a month. Mark is told he'll never walk normally again and likely will never surf again either.

"I won't lie to you, it was a tough time spending three months in the hospital," Mark confides. "At times I'd drift back thinking negatively again about what happened and where I was at, but then I'd think of that kid. He really helped me."[5]

Over the coming months Mark would undergo multiple surgeries to help repair the damage in his leg, but his prognosis would remain poor. "They said I was going to have nerve damage for life, which means I can't lift my foot anymore. Basically, I can't lift my foot up, it just hangs down."[6]

He returned to his beachside home where he was forced to remain couch bound as his injuries healed. He'd spend the next six months confined in a physical purgatory reflecting on his future. "I couldn't even look at it," he says of the ocean outside his front window. "It was tough and I had plenty of dark days."[7]

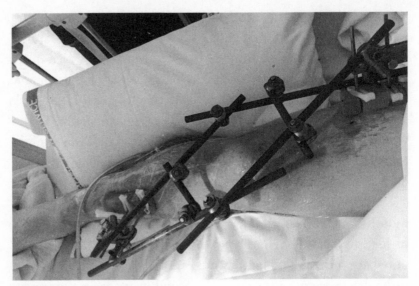

Mark Mathew's extensive leg injuries　　　　　*Courtesy of AIP Group, Mark Mathews*

But through it all, Mark kept reflecting back on Jason and thinking how much worse it could have been. He began his physical therapy in earnest and started to see progress. During his final surgery, doctors were able to move tendons around in his foot and lengthen his Achilles tendon so his foot wouldn't drop anymore. It was a game changer.

In late December 2017, 14 months after his career-ending injury, Mark paddled out at Maroubra, his home break in Sydney, and with the help from a custom brace stabilizing his ankle, caught some small waves on his longboard. It was a far cry from the monster faces that have defined his big-wave-surfing career, but in many ways these small waves were just as meaningful and important.

"Now I wake up every day and check the swell forecast again. I'm only looking for one-foot waves, but still. My life's gone back to revolving around weather forecasts, which is such an exciting way to live."[8]

Mark's improvement has proven much faster than even he thought possible, and his aspirations have grown. "I wasn't supposed to be doing that for another few months, but it felt really good," he explains. "I feel like I'm going to get back way quicker than I thought."[9] He's begun talking about surfing giants again and doing what everyone, including himself, thought was completely impossible just a year ago. "I'll probably focus on the big deep-water wave stuff, like Jaws in Hawaii or Nazaré in Portugal, and maybe a couple big wave events."[10]

The very suggestion of riding waves like this again is not just inspiring but frankly astonishing. These are massive faces of water unlike most of us could ever imagine. Nazaré, for example, has reached a height of 100 feet. That's a 10-story building sweeping across the ocean surface.

But that is the mindset of Mark Mathews. For him, anything is possible. What allows Mark to have the mental wherewithal to claw back from catastrophic injury and still have the fortitude to remain committed to the very thing that has hurt him so badly? How does he do it? What are the secrets to Mark's success?

Changing Your Perspective with Cognitive Reappraisal

Imagine yourself in Mark's position just prior to meeting the boy Jason in the hospital. You've just sustained the most significant set of injuries of your life, and you're facing the reality that your career as a big wave surfer might be over. What emotions do you think you'd be feeling?

Truth be told, if you weren't swimming in negative emotions, there'd be something wrong. You'd certainly be feeling angry at your misfortune and fearful that you may never surf again. You'd likely be berating yourself for choosing to surf even though you knew you were still hurt, and you'd be feeling sadness for burdening the people who care about you with the angst of seeing you in pain. Lying in your hospital bed, you'd feel the flood of negative emotions that any normal human being would feel after experiencing such a profound trauma. And then you'd meet Jason.

This young boy, who had suffered a profound injury of his own, would briefly come into your life. He would provide you with an opportunity to cope. Mark recognized that coping mechanism right away and immediately began using it to help in his own recovery. Would you be able to recognize it as quickly and know what to do?

Adventure athletes like surfer Mark Mathews who seek out extreme challenge invariably find their fair share of serious misfortune, but all of us, no matter our predisposition toward risk-taking, will face some sort of difficulty in our lives. Setbacks can come in a myriad of forms. It may be the death of a loved one or the loss of a job. It may be a physical trauma like what Mark endured crashing on that reef, or it may be an emotional one as we ruminate on something bad that happened. Or it may be something less serious but still upsetting: a poor performance review, not meeting a quarterly target, or being looked over for a promotion or another role. Regardless of how a challenge manifests, we will all face setbacks in our lives. The real question is how will we deal with those setbacks.

Irrespective of one's natural capacity to cope with setbacks, research in the fields of neuroscience and psychology point to a key coping mechanism that can be employed by everyone to manage physical and emotional stress. It's called cognitive reappraisal.

Cognitive reappraisal is our ability to consciously manage our emotional experiences and responses to a setback or challenge and to transform the negative emotions we feel into more positive ones. For example, being laid off from your job is often a traumatic experience accompanied by negative feelings around inadequacy and inability. A certain level of realistic introspection is always warranted in such a circumstance, but all too often the negative experiences you feel will decrease your self-confidence and hinder your ability to rebound from the layoff and find a new job. Using cognitive reappraisal may be as simple as recognizing that the job was not an ideal fit between you and the company, and that you've been now given the opportunity to find a better position at an organization that will allow you to bring your strengths to the table. It's all about stopping a negative response from overloading your brain's rational circuits and keeping your head clear. Cognitive reappraisal lets us not only acknowledge and reduce our emotional response to a negative situation, but it also changes our perspective on that situation by letting us take a step back and add a positive spin to whatever challenge we're facing. It's a very powerful coping mechanism and one that Mark Mathew's story embodies well.

Salespeople: The Corporate Masters of Cognitive Reappraisal

As important as cognitive reappraisal is for big wave surfer Mark Mathews in dealing with the big waves and setbacks he faces, the ability to reframe a situation is equally essential for the business professional. And one doesn't have to look very hard in the work environment to see it in action.

Recently, we met up with Shevaun Lee, vice president of relationship management at BetterUp, a startup technology company located in San Francisco that brings personalized professional coaching to the corporate marketplace. Lee has been the top salesperson at BetterUp for the past three years and recently accepted Aragon Research's Women in Tech 18 award for sales. She is a peak performer in the sales arena yet remarkably, doesn't see herself as a salesperson.

"I see myself as a talent practitioner who had the good fortune to stumble across a tiny startup with a product that has the potential to change the way businesses think about driving strategy through people. How can you not want to sell that?"

Prior to joining BetterUp, Shevaun had spent 10 years as a management consultant for the multinational professional services firm of Deloitte, where she worked as a strategist solving challenging client problems. She wouldn't have called herself a salesperson in that role. But now with a different set of goals and objectives, in the formal role of a salesperson, she intuitively responded to her unforeseen sales prowess in the way successful salespeople often do, by reframing the situation. Instead of seeing herself as being a talented salesperson, she instead framed her unanticipated aptitude for selling as being the outcome of having the good fortune of finding an up-and-coming startup with a great product she felt compelled to sell. In her mind, through her reframing, she wasn't a salesperson at all, but rather an advocate of something that was bigger than her.

Shevaun understands, from both her sales and her talent strategist experience, that salespeople are keen cognitive reappraisers. "We have to reframe when we get told 'no' from a customer and think about the problem that we're trying to solve, not the product that we're trying to sell." It's an approach reflected in the sales industry as a whole as the entire profession shifts from a *product*-based to a *solution*-based focus.

Salespeople are the modern masters of cognitive reappraisal and embody, as author and business thinker Daniel Pink calls it, a sense of buoyancy. In his book *To Sell Is Human*, Pink describes buoyancy as "the capacity to stay afloat on what one salesman calls an 'ocean of rejection.'" It's the "grittiness of spirit and sunniness of outlook" that allows great salespeople to habitually use cognitive reappraisal. They swim through a tumultuous ocean of rejection and remain afloat by not only believing in what they are selling, but by looking at it in a positive light. Go find a successful salesperson in your company and take them out for lunch. Listen to the language they use in framing the challenges they have in meeting their targets. You will no doubt find them peppered with positive and optimistic stories of how they are planning to exceed their goals.

As straightforward as it may sound in theory, using cognitive reappraisal can be very difficult when you're struggling. It's easy to say "look at the bright side of life" when you're not facing the darkness of a serious setback, but being able to do it in exactly those moments is where the power of reframing lies. As Mark Mathews said himself, "I like to call it forced cognitive reappraisal. Like something made that happen. It's very hard to do. It's very hard to tell someone who is going through something tough."

In the adventure world, Mark's story of a chance meeting with an injured boy sparked his ability to distance himself from his current situation. From his perspective, it was a forced reappraisal. He was confronted with someone going through a tougher challenge than his own, and it caused him to take a step back from his situation and gain a broader perspective. There is little doubt Mark was feeling a series of complex emotions in response to his leg injury, as traumatic as it was, but in that instance, he was able to step back and reappraise his own situation. He objectively realized his situation was much less severe than his young fan's trauma, which had left him paralyzed and confined to a wheelchair. In an instant, Mark could reappraise his own situation and use it to move forward, positively reframing his injury and his future recovery.

Was this Mark's first try at cognitive reappraisal? Absolutely not. Big wave surfing is a very dangerous sport, and Mark has had to face many difficult setbacks over the years. Mark's ability to positively reframe a situation both on and off the waves has come with lots of practice, and this practice developed a habit of cognitive reappraisal that served him well when he needed it most. Without realizing it, he has trained himself to look at the bright side of life and it has become a habit. And Mark's habit of cognitively reappraising a situation isn't limited to only after setbacks either; he routinely reframes challenges before they happen as well.

As mentioned at the start of the chapter, before heading out into huge surf, Mark goes through intense mental preparation, scenario-planning the direst outcomes he could face while on the water, in order to best plan his responses. As Mark puts it, "Worst-case scenario is if I get knocked unconscious, not breathing, bleeding, even to the extent of bringing a defibrillator on one of the boats if my heart stops beating, doing all this, doing all the underwater training, and all the preparation that makes the scary situation on the day less so. It makes it possible for me to go 'OK, I can handle it.'"

By cognitively reappraising the danger, Mark anticipates about how he'll respond to situations before they happen and reframes these scenarios into less-terrifying problems that he can solve now. Reframing an unexpected outcome as something that could happen and then planning how it might be solved before it happens is the practice of cognitive reappraisal before a traumatic event. Mark does this all the time.

Individuals who habitually use cognitive reappraisal see positive downstream impacts, both mentally and physically, from it. They deal with negative setbacks more easily and tend to look at the bright side of situations. They ruminate on their missteps less and bounce back quicker from their daily setbacks and mistakes. Some studies have even shown that cognitive reappraisal helps strengthen personal relationships, improve well-being, and lower stress.[11] The science points to the benefits of cognitive reappraisal; the challenge is making it a habit.

One effective way to help make cognitive reappraisal a habit is by training yourself to practice it when you're faced with smaller challenges in your day-to-day experience. For example, you're leading a presentation on a conference call with a large group of people and you make a mistake. You're called out publicly by a coworker, or even worse, your boss, in front of everyone on the call. You can't see their responses, but you can imagine others on the phone shaking their heads in disappointment and irritation. As your stomach churns and embarrassment settles in, you fumble for a response, but it doesn't come. The anxiety and anger of being called out has hijacked you. It's time to reappraise.

Instead of presuming your critic to be a detractor, let's flip the situation and assume positive intent. The person who was on the other end of the line wasn't intending to make you feel anxious or angry, but rather intended to add to the discussion and make sure the details were right. Their aim was to help propel the conversation and the goal toward the same outcome you are working toward. By reframing the narrative in situations like this, you can reduce the negative emotional impact you feel and improve the clarity of your thinking.

Building the habit of using cognitive reappraisal in day-to-day scenarios like this will help you draw upon it naturally when more acute moments of stress and setback arise. It's like developing fitness through an exercise program; it's there when you need it. We all accept that emotional regulation and cognitive reappraisal in the moment of extreme stress is something that is very hard to employ, and therefore we need to build a habit to use it so, when something serious does happen, we naturally do the right things to deal with it.

How Does Cognitive Reappraisal Work?

Cognitive reappraisal has been studied extensively over the last decade and a half, and the findings suggest that the process of reframing a negative situation in a positive light fundamentally changes your brain. In one prominent study published in the *Journal of Cognitive Neuroscience* in 2002, Columbia University neuroscientist Kevin Ochsner and his team found that teaching a person to think of a negative stimulus in a positive light leads to a measurable neurological change in how they emotionally experience and react to this negative stimulus. The study employed functional magnetic resonance imaging, fMRI, a tool that measures blood flow to different areas of the brain, to look at the way neural systems changed when a person cognitively reappraised a given situation or stimuli and it came up with fascinating results.

The study showed that when a subject positively reframed a negative scene, their brain actually changed. Their prefrontal cortex, the area of the brain integral to one's cognitive behavior and emotional self-regulation, was activated by their reframing of the situation, while their amygdala, the area of the brain associated with fear and anxiety, saw a reduction in activity. The study suggested that by thinking about a negative experience in a different way, you have the capacity to reduce the fear and anxiety associated with that negative stimuli and promote emotional regulation. You have the capability to teach yourself to overcome negative stress and create a positive outcome, changing your brain in the process.

Putting reappraisal into practice can be most challenging when it's related to career advancement. Trying to paint a positive picture when you have been passed over for a great role or promotion often stirs up negative emotions toward those in the decision-making position and can be very difficult. "Why didn't they choose me?" you may wonder.

So you've been passed over for that great promotion and you're really upset. Who wouldn't be? The first thing that you'll experience is an emotional processing of the disappointment: you'll be angry, hurt, deflated. This is perfectly normal and is OK. But then, all too frequently, you'll begin the detrimental downward spiral of second-guessing your value, your capabilities, and your fit within the company. This, too, is normal but is not OK. This is the moment when you need to put cognitive reappraisal into action. Acknowledge that you're having an emotional reaction to not being chosen, and try to pull back from it and look at it rationally. Begin to reframe the situation. For example, you may not have been chosen this time, but this may give you the opportunity to gain additional skill and mastery to be ready for the next time. Or you treat the outcome as a wake-up call to go after the roles you really want and for you to demonstrate your skills more clearly. However you do it, once you reframe the setbacks in a more positive light, you'll reduce your negative stress and build your emotional intelligence in the process.

Thinking back to Mark Mathews, what's interesting about him is that when you first meet him, you're struck by his cheerful and positive outlook on life. Mark's the quintessential "surfer dude" on the surface, but his easygoing nature belies his deeply thoughtful and reflective approach to his work. It makes you wonder how someone who puts himself in such stressful and dangerous situations can be so positive and relaxed about it. Does building a habit of cognitive reappraisal have other wider-reaching positive impacts on our life? Can we all adopt Mark's sunny attitude with a little practice? The research seems to suggest so.

Mark Mathews negotiating the infamous step on a massive barrel wave at Shipstern Bluff off the coast of Tasmania, Australia   *Courtesy of AIP Group, Mark Mathews*

There appears to be a link between protection against depression and the ability to cognitively reappraise traumatic situations. In one sample study led by Allison Troy of the University of Denver, women with a high ability to cognitively reappraise stressful situations, cognitive reappraisal ability (CRA), exhibited fewer symptoms of depression than those with low CRA, suggesting that regulation abilities may be an important moderator of the link between stressful events and depression symptoms.[12] In another study, individuals who successfully down-regulated negative affect by reshaping their thoughts about a potentially emotional situation showed augmented activity in the prefrontal cortex (PFC) with attenuated activity in the amygdala.[13] Simply put, they boosted their thinking brain up while dialing their emotional brain down. The research indicates that an individual's ability to positively reappraise situations in a mindful but relaxed state helps them better deal with stress, anxiety, and depression and leads to a healthier outlook on life. This outlook has tangible business outcomes. After all, when you can better deal with the strong emotions of work in a more effective and emotionally intelligent way, you are more productive and a model for how a leader behaves in the face of adversity.

How Do You Use Cognitive Reappraisal?

Mark felt that his cognitive reappraisal of his trauma was an involuntary action on his part. From his perspective, he would not have been able to reappraise his situation without meeting Jason and seeing his challenges in comparison to his own. In Mark's own words, it felt like "forced cognitive reappraisal." We beg to differ.

In our minds, Mark wasn't forced into a reframing but naturally gravitated toward it when he met Jason. Mark was already familiar with cognitive reappraisal and had made reframing a habitual response. He reframed his trauma quickly because he had trained himself to do so. Mark wasn't forced to cognitively reappraise his situation; he was triggered to do it. Habit pulled the trigger.

Cognitive reappraisal is hard. We've all struggled with looking on the bright side of a challenging situation only to be too overwhelmed to get very far. To successfully use cognitive reappraisal when you critically need it, you need to practice at it when you don't. The way to do this is by reframing simple stressors in your daily life and building upon them, making reappraisal a natural go-to when things get difficult and making it a habit. As the studies show if you train yourself to do it, your brain will follow.

Another equally important part of reappraisal is being able to anticipate and reappraise prior to a traumatic event.[14] We can't predict future challenges and setbacks, of course, but what we can do is be proactive and initiate reappraisal right at the start of an emotion-inducing event. When we feel strong emotions, we get physiological feedback immediately—it's what makes us human. Our breathing becomes shallow, our heart races, our palms sweat, our stomach churns. By understanding what's happening and recognizing these physiological symptoms at the early stages of an event, we can reappraise situations and lessen the emotional impact. But we need to be right on top of it.

If we miss these symptoms at the early stage, we quickly move into something called the emotional "point of no return," where your emotions become fully activated and reappraisal becomes exceptionally difficult.[15] Practicing this anticipatory regulation during small and low-stakes stressors allows you to understand your own point of no return and pull you back from it.

Consider a mistake you may have recently made at work. Maybe you copied everyone on an email when you shouldn't have, or you lost a big sales deal with an important client; whatever it is, you screwed up. As human beings we are naturally wired for negativity, and our natural tendency is to beat ourselves up over our errors. All too often we somehow see ourselves as bad for doing what human beings do all the time—making a mistake. Consider the lens of reframing like a big wave surfer, and let's try a different approach.

Suppose you lost a sales deal. First, acknowledge the physical response at the onset of the setback. You feel the heat of the blood flow making your face flush with tension. This is your first indication that your body is preparing for an emotional response. Next, assess the emotion you are feeling and pick out a word that best describes this emotion and label it. You've lost the deal and you may feel disappointment, anger, or sadness; whatever it is, acknowledge it and label it. Labeling the emotion is one of the tools to reengage the language center of the prefrontal cortex, your rational brain, to get you into a mode of thinking rather than feeling. By doing this you are redirecting blood flow away from your amygdala, the area of the brain associated with fear and anxiety processing, and moving it to the prefrontal cortex where you emotionally self-regulate.

Now with your thinking brain turned back on, find the positive or learning experience related to the loss of the sales deal. Maybe you'll aim to get to know your competition better before making a proposal, or you'll be more forthright in your questioning during a sales meeting. Again, whatever it is, present yourself with new actionable behaviors to address the mistake or challenge you faced. By taking action like this, you begin to see the mistake you made as an opportunity to learn and grow rather than as a case of inadequacy.

Putting Cognitive Reappraisal into Action for Yourself

The ability to cognitively reappraise is a key tool in the executive's high-performance toolkit. We humans are nothing if not adaptive, and this capacity, at least in part, depends on our ability to regulate responses to life's affective pushes and pulls.[16] Cognitive reappraisal allows us to maneuver around negative roadblocks that hinder our path forward. It's a tremendously useful skill to have, but one that needs to become habit to be effective. Here are three ways to practice building your own cognitive reappraisal abilities:

1. **Start small and practice.** As humans, we are wired for survival, and as such, looking at the world through a positive lens goes against our natural instincts. Start small with cognitive reappraisal; otherwise, your colleagues and family might wonder if perhaps you've been replaced by a strange sunshine-and-rainbows body double. Think differently about a small challenge you have, and reframe it into something that excites or energizes you. When you make an error, reframe that into what you can learn from the experience instead of beating yourself up over it.

2. **Learn to recognize your emotions.** We tend to stifle our emotions, particularly at work and if they are negative. Learning to recognize your emotional reactions while they are happening is stuff of experts. To start on the path of recognizing your emotions, begin by writing it down. Expressive writing has many benefits, particularly around improving mood and boosting memory,[17] but it also allows you to better identify your emotions and reflect on situations that may trigger these emotions more acutely. Mark Mathews uses journaling often to "get it out of your head and write it down" to keep himself calm when stressed. Try recapping your day with 5 to 10 minutes of writing about what happened and how you reacted for a week. Do this at the end of the day to allow yourself time to reflect and sleep off any negativity.

After a week, see if you are better able to anticipate what emotions occur and why. The physical act of writing not only allows you to reflect on what might be emotional patterns in your behavior but also engages the language cortex of your brain. It lets you redirect your mental energy to rationally understand your emotions rather than just feeling them. Writing forces people to reconstrue whatever is troubling them and find new meaning in it.[18]

3. **Make cognitive reappraisal a habit.** Once you have started small and done some expressive writing, work on integrating cognitive reappraisal as a habit. Reframing those small and less consequential daily negative situations, challenges, and problems actually eases the load you put on your brain. Whether it's being gentler on yourself when you send that incorrect email or being easier on the barista who has mistaken your coffee order, reappraising the ripples of everyday life will help you be ready to face those bigger waves when they roll in.

When Mark Mathews was a young man, he had a simple insight that reframed the rest of his life. He was returning home from an overseas journey and purchased a copy of the Dalai Lama's *The Art of Happiness* as a gift for his mother. "My mom is super spiritual," says Mark. "I would never have read this book normally. I thought this stuff was always silly, but I had time on the plane and I read it. It was a turning point for me. I realized that being happy was up to me." The Dalai Lama espouses that happiness is a perceived reality dictated by your own mind and not by external conditions, circumstances, or events. He believes that if we are able to train our hearts and minds to be positive and happy, we will be happy.

A switch was flipped in Mark. He understood that his happiness as a human being—the underpinning of his burgeoning career as a professional surfer, the foundation of everything that was him—depended solely on his perception of it. How he perceived it depended entirely on how he framed it. It was an early lesson in cognitive reappraisal that charted his life forever.

The ability to cognitively reappraise is an exceptionally valuable skill, but as simple and straightforward as it appears, it requires dedication and practice to become routine. For those individuals like Mark Mathews who do make it routine, for those individuals who naturally employ cognitive reappraisal when they face the myriad of life's challenges, the outcomes are immediate, profound, and life changing. Do yourself a favor and enhance your high-performance toolkit. Let cognitive reappraisal become part of your life.

CHAPTER 2

Grit

The Passion to Prevail

t was January 7, 2006, and Paul Gleeson and Tori Holmes were at their wits' end. They were taking part in the Woodvale Transatlantic Rowing Race and were adrift in the middle of the Atlantic Ocean aboard their tiny 23-foot rowing boat named *Christina*. It was their 39th day at sea, and the young couple was over a thousand miles from land. Three days earlier, their water-maker began to fail and they had been rationing water ever since. A water-maker is critical for survival on a journey like this, because it extracts salt from the ocean water to make it drinkable. Without it, Paul and Tori would die from thirst.

"We decided to continue rowing, limiting ourselves to five liters of water a day," lamented Tori. "It was torturous." The two rowers had a freshwater reserve on the boat acting as ballast. But the supply was limited, and as they used it up, the boat became less seaworthy. Removing ballast from a boat is like clipping the wings off a plane; the more you remove, the less stable it gets. A boat without ballast begs to be flipped, and being flipped is the nightmare of every ocean rower. Clinging to an overturned boat in the middle of the Atlantic a thousand miles from shore was a horror no human being would ever want to face. The prospect was as terrifying as it was perilous, but it was something Paul and Tori would now have to consider.

"We rowed for two hours in the blistering heat, allowing ourselves less than one-eighth of a liter, we're talking sips, here, per shift," explains Tori. "All I wanted to do was grab the whole bottle and chug it down." But she didn't. The two novice adventurers kept rowing, kept rationing, and stubbornly kept moving forward.

"I never thought it would end," says Paul. "We were so hot, so thirsty, it all started to feel so unbearable. And then finally the call came." It was the moment they had been waiting for and it took three days to come. "The water-maker company got

Paul Gleeson and Tori Holmes completing their row across the Atlantic Ocean

Courtesy of Paul Gleeson

through to us on our satellite phone," Paul explains. "A technician told us that the fitting on the side of the boat that sucks in the ocean water wasn't staying continuously under water. He said air was getting into the system and we were going to have to bleed it to make it work." In heaving seas, the two adventurers would take shifts working on the desalinator, following the detailed technical instructions given to them until finally, after another two full days, they got it working again. It was a momentous occasion for Paul and Tori. They overcame a near journey-ending disaster and were now back on track. But instead of celebrating, the hapless duo didn't have time to reflect on how vulnerable they were. A huge tropical storm had descended upon them, and they had nowhere to hide.

"I looked up and it was as though a wall was rushing toward me," exclaimed Tori, bewildered by the speed the storm had enveloped them. "Everywhere you looked there were huge breaking waves, curling over each other. As I clenched tightly to the oars that bounced up and down, from side to side, it felt like I was performing in a rodeo, not rowing a boat."

Tori Holmes facing a huge swell in the Atlantic   *Courtesy of Paul Gleeson*

It took no time before the sea became a cordillera of steel gray peaks, all in motion, all in disarray. Mountains of water colliding, building into frothing monsters, and collapsing again. The ocean surface was whipped into a fury as Paul and Tori, aboard their tiny boat *Christina*, realized they were now at the mercy of the ocean. "I saw a rush of water coming directly for me, like an animal jumping right at my face," explained Tori. "It launched me from my seat, threw me down, and nearly washed me overboard. And then I could see the boat coming over top of me."

As the *Christina* began to roll, the oars whirled about and swept out like outriggers to help her remain upright. The oars bent horribly under the weight of the boat and quickly burst from their oarlocks, but the momentary halt was enough to prevent *Christina* from capsizing. It had been Tori's turn on the oars, and Paul was asleep in the cabin when the wave hit. He awoke to a loud thud and a terrifying scream, and only caught a glimpse of Tori's feet in the air awash in white foam through the plexiglass cabin door before she disappeared from view. "Are you all right, Pup?" he shouted to Tori as he clambered onto the deck. "I think I've broken my ribs," she replied, barely able to speak. She was still lying where she'd been thrown. "I can't breathe."

Tori began to panic. "Every time I took a breath, a rush of pain would shoot up my esophagus. I started to feel lightness in my head. The more anxious I became, the more pain I felt. In this moment, I was four years old again; all I wanted was my mom."

It would take Paul over an hour of continuous calling via satellite phone before he would make contact with their expedition doctor on land. Tori had reached her breaking point. They were told that her injury likely included a bruised gallbladder in addition to a broken rib. They were told that for her rib injury, there was nothing to do but rest, but for the pain in her esophagus, there was a remedy. "The clever doctor suggested eating toothpaste," says Paul with a grin. "Tori was experiencing a severe case of acid reflux from her gallbladder injury. Toothpaste is filled with calcium and it neutralizes the acid. She wasn't thrilled about the idea, but she had to do it."

Through the entire vexing ordeal, Tori thought of her mom. "I knew if I could just get through to hear the calming sound of her voice, the inner confidence she brings to my life would calm me down."

Strange things happen in bizarre moments, and thousands of miles away in the frozen heartland of Canada's Northwest Territories, Tori's father awoke in the middle of the night from a nightmare. He saw his young daughter with her head underwater and a look of terror on her face. He bolted up and went to his phone to send a text to his daughter who was somewhere out in the middle of the Atlantic.

"There he was, in spirit, to my rescue, as always," Tori explains. "So I took the quote and recited those words every minute of every shift for the next two weeks, putting myself in an almost trance-like zone. In the end I did what I had to do."

"Push through the pain, face the fear to Valhalla and back, you're a Viking!"

There's only one word that describes what Paul and Tori were displaying throughout this ordeal: grit. The word describes a very special capability that allowed both of them to muster the courage to keep moving through one of the most challenging moments of their lives.

Grit is the engine of human accomplishment.[1] It is the capacity to dig deep and do whatever it takes—sacrifice, struggle, and suffer—to achieve a worthy goal in the best of ways.[2]

Grit is the combination of passion and perseverance that, according to the celebrated researcher and professor of psychology Angela Duckworth, is the key to outstanding achievement. In her groundbreaking book, *Grit: The Power of Passion and Perseverance*, Duckworth explores the special quality that both Paul and Tori are displaying on their row across the Atlantic Ocean. She examines a wide range of grit paragons and concludes that having a higher level of grit predicts a variety of academic and vocational outcomes over and above skills and intelligence. Duckworth discovers through her exhaustive research that exhibiting higher levels of grit predicts greater achievement outcomes and highlights. She demonstrates that grittier people exhibit increased educational attainment, fewer career changes, higher retention rates at notoriously challenging institutions like the US Military Academy, and increased success at the Scripps National Spelling Bee competition. Whether you're 14-year-old spelling bee champion Karthik Nemmani grappling with the word *koinonia*, or Paul and Tori facing the violent wrath of an angry ocean, grittier people always seem to have the upper hand. Duckworth's research indicates grit is an integral component of high performance, and this is no better exemplified than in the adventure world where its existence, or lack of, could mean the difference between life and death. We have seen this firsthand in business as well, particularly when individuals and teams deal with long periods of organizational change.

These days, grit is a mandatory attribute for leaders facing the relentless speed of transformation in the modern business world. The majority of professionals face nonstop cycles of change to their business models, to their organizations, and to their industries. From large-scale mergers and acquisitions to digital transformation and global market upheavals, people are becoming ever more overwhelmed and "change-fatigued." They're experiencing continuous transformations and can find themselves unable to keep up. Yet all too often, the companies they're employed by provide little support in helping them managing this change at either the personal or organizational level.

So how do you cope with this onslaught? How do you sustain personal and organizational performance while dealing with up and down cycles, market fluctuations, new technologies, information overload, and continued transformational change? Like Paul and Tori, who as rank novices faced down the Atlantic Ocean in a row boat and somehow made it across against all odds, you employ a capability that lets you do what you need to do to get the job done. You use grit.

Let's take a closer look at how we can build this essential capacity.

Fake It Till You Make It: The Stories We Tell Ourselves

Jennifer's career decisions had always been very measured and responsible. As a successful vice president at a large global financial services company, she had enthusiastically taken on a variety of academic and business challenges and used wisdom, learning, and seeking advice to help bolster her career.

Like many professional women, she assumed she could apply the same logical approach to having her first child. She was independent, resourceful, and confident she could handle this life-changing event. And why not? She approached the task as she did most changes in her life. Jennifer made detailed plans. She took classes and read countless books. She was poised enough that she even declined help from her mom, who offered to fly across the country to join her for the birth. Jennifer was ready for her first child.

After a successful birth, Jennifer and her husband left the hospital with their new bundle of joy and returned home feeling buoyed and self-assured. Like many other parents of newborns, the shock to the system came soon after. The dream ended when they closed the front door. As babies do, their newborn son began to cry. And cry he did, nonstop, for hours and hours, unrelenting and inconsolable. No matter what she did, Jennifer couldn't soothe him and make him stop crying. Through all her planning and all her reading, she was not prepared for this. She felt powerless and exasperated, and when the nurse from the maternity ward called to check in on her, the floodgates holding back her emotions finally tore open. "I have no idea what I'm doing!" she sobbed into the phone, "How did you let me leave the hospital? I want to come back!"

It was a humbling moment for Jennifer. The self-reliant and successful business leader had lost all her confidence and was now second-guessing everything. It became glaringly clear that she actually knew very little about motherhood, and her infant son needed her more than anything else in the world. All her planning and prepping hadn't prepared her for the job, but now she was facing it nonetheless. The independent and strong Jennifer who had everything under control realized she needed help. It was a rude awakening for her, but she changed the narrative of her story to embrace support and kept on doing what every young mother has to do—she kept on faking it until she made it. She reached out to accept help, asked for advice, and tried a variety of methods with varying levels of success, adapting as she went.

Fast-forward several years later, and Jennifer faced that same draining fear of the unknown in her professional life. The financial services industry was going through a significant and unexpected change to a critical part of her company's business model. The company had a lot of work to do to adapt to those changes—they were global and far-reaching, and they would require massive upheaval to the systems and processes already in place. It was a daunting global project, and Jennifer was selected to be part of the core team that would rally stakeholders from around the world to get the herculean effort done.

Although excited about the opportunity, the same doubts about her capabilities began to creep in, "How could the organization think I could do this? There's no book on how to handle such a massive change! Am I really the right person for this job?" But then Jennifer the professional began to think like Jennifer the mom. She reframed the story in her head and took the same steps in her job that allowed her to be a better mom. She accepted help from others, tapped into her trusted network of experts, and focused on her small wins. She recognized that, just like in motherhood, she couldn't plan for every challenge she'd face, but she could eventually overcome them by having the courage to learn from others, seek advice, and keep going. She applied those same tactics, building on her past experiences and applying similar solutions to her new challenge, and they worked.

Being able to "fake it until you make it" is one of the key ways to work through impostor syndrome, or the psychological pattern in which you doubt your accomplishments and have a persistent internalized fear of being exposed as a fraud. Jennifer's ability to use "fake it until you make it" allowed her to remain confident, to keep reminding herself that she is smart, capable, and accomplished during the process of learning something new and intimidating. Over time the faking is replaced by a more genuine confidence and self-belief. This changes the internal narrative. The "I can't do this" is replaced by "you got this."

Paul and Tori faced impostor syndrome the moment they decided to row across the Atlantic Ocean. Neither had any rowing experience, and on the surface, they had no realistic prospect at succeeding at what they had set out to do. They had only one real adventure under their belts—a cycling journey across Australia—and that journey was very commonplace in comparison to rowing the Atlantic. Having never rowed before, they were about to undertake one of the most difficult challenges a rower could ever face. They were faking it and they knew it.

Very often, impostor syndrome manifests itself as a loud soundtrack playing in our heads, reminding us we're not good enough or capable enough, that someone else has made a terrible mistake of putting us in the situation we're in. That we're about to be "found out" for our lack of expertise or experience. We reinforce this thinking by listening to that negative internal voice and giving it a chance to influence our thinking. By nature, we have a tendency toward negative thinking. It's in our DNA. Being on the lookout for negativity is a fundamental survival mechanism that helps keep us alert and safe and lets us recognize and avoid dangerous situations. Our negative tendency got us to where we are today, and its effectiveness is proven out by our success as a species. But things have changed for the majority of us. Marauding war parties and hungry predators are rarely a major concern for us these days. Yet our brains remain on high alert. In its search for negativity, our brains readily associate a workplace dilemma, something far from being truly dangerous, as unfamiliar or risky and elicit a similar fight-or-flight response of something much more perilous. This is a problem. Our natural tendency toward negativity supercharges the negative soundtrack playing in our head, and before long, our imposter syndrome in these scenarios can become overwhelming and debilitating.

Silencing the loud and constant voice of impostor syndrome and replacing it with a positive narrative is one of the key elements to building grit. It's about the story you tell yourself and the strength of the internal *locus of control* you build. Locus of control is an idea created by psychologist Julian B. Rotter in 1966. It describes the extent to which you believe you have power over the events in your life versus blaming outside forces for things that happen to you. It influences the story you tell yourself about the situation you find yourself in. If you are struggling with impostor syndrome, that internal story can be loud and negative and it takes a lot of effort to silence it or rewrite the narrative into something positive.

For Paul and Tori, the way they checked their imposter syndrome and silenced the negative thoughts in their heads was to smother them with more positive ones. Each employed a number of conspicuous cues to put themselves into a more positive headspace. Some were revealed by chance, like the note from Tori's father that became a mantra for her, but others were more intentional. Paul and Tori had painted the saying, *"Pain is temporary, quitting lasts forever,"* across the top of the bulkhead leading into their aft cabin and stared at it every time they rowed. They knew the words of this saying would resonate with them and would give them an added boost when times got tough. They did this intentionally. Paul and Tori secured images of friends and family to the to the ceiling of the cabin where they slept. Every time they woke, the first thing they saw were the people who loved them and supported them unconditionally. The images raised their spirits and reaffirmed their feelings of purpose and resolve for their row. In the small footwell where they stepped each time they entered and exited through the cabin door, they affixed a small ceramic tile that read, *"The difficult we do immediately, the impossible takes a little longer."* Again, like the other reminders and touch points on their boat, the words would remind them every time they entered and exited the cabin that their task at hand required monumental perseverance. Whether they realised it or not, Paul and Tori were priming their minds at both a conscious and subconscious level to bring about an emotive state that would help them do what they needed to do.

A quote written on the cabin of Paul Gleeson and Tori Holmes's boat   *Courtesy of Paul Gleeson*

Intention begets action. Paul and Tori recognized that their inner self-critics were going to be ever-present companions on the journey and took deliberate steps beforehand to quiet them. Inner negative voices can often derail an effort even before it gets started and bolster imposter syndrome. Paul and Tori knew this and took action to address it.

And just like Paul and Tori, Jennifer, the professional and the mom, took steps to address her negative inner voice by having the courage to learn from others, to seek their advice, and to keep going. She applied the same tactics she learned as a young mother to help her through the challenges of her professional career. Whether you're an adventurer or not, you can take steps to address imposter syndrome before it hinders your performance.

American psychiatrist and researcher Aaron T. Beck, recognized globally as the father of cognitive therapy, has studied the way our thoughts affect us for over six decades and his groundbreaking theories have shaped the way we look at and treat clinical depression. Beck suggested that it was an individual's subjective interpretation of any given life event that gave rise to their feelings and behaviors around it, not the event itself. He proposed that a psychiatrist could talk directly to a patient about what was bothering them and address their self-talk in their treatment. He felt that regardless of background and past life experience, we can all learn to observe and discern our negative thinking and change our behavior accordingly. Paul and Tori were taking it one step further by anticipating the negative soundtrack around their imposter syndrome and took steps to counteract it.

Eleven years after Paul embarked on his row across the Atlantic Ocean, he found himself studying the psychological elements of grit and its foundations as part of his own psychological research. For his dissertation, Paul conducted research in the corporate world around the impact that internal locus of control and well-being had on people's perception of their own grit. He found that the internal story we tell ourselves is not only relevant in building grit but also can be directly influenced by our writing and reflections on our own emotions and reactions. Paul found that by writing about one's own emotions and behaviors, individuals garnered a stronger sense of emotional well-being.

Taking the time to really look at our life experiences and the stories created around those experiences is one of the lessons author and leadership trainer Laurie Sudbrink discusses in her paper *Leveraging Grit for Leadership Success.*[3] Reflecting on our stories can be difficult because ego often gets in the way. But the ability to be more human and to reflect on the emotions we feel in tough situations helps us rewrite those stories into learning experiences rather than failure events. Too often, we feel the need to perform to perfection showing no weakness. Ironically it's when we're more transparent and vulnerable, when we show positive intent, when we demonstrate a desire to learn and grow that people connect with us better and trust us more. We become a stronger and more impactful leader by embracing the power of our own vulnerability.

What's the story you want to tell? How can you fake it till you make it?

Building the Fire

The idea to row the Atlantic Ocean came to Paul as a question from an old schoolmate, Shane O'Neill, in August 2004. It was the end of a late evening on the town and Shane was saying good-bye to Paul and Tori as they were headed home in a taxi. Paul was closing the passenger door when Shane leaned in and asked him in a lowered voice, "Would you have an interest in rowing across the Atlantic Ocean?" recounts Paul. "His tone was unusually cool, like someone suggesting a game of golf."

"Are you serious?" Paul replied, instantly taken by the idea.

Tori hadn't heard what Shane had said and Paul didn't share it. His mind was racing. "As the taxi drove us home, I said nothing to Tori," he remembers. "I had never rowed a boat and had no ocean experience whatsoever, but I was captivated. I didn't know why I was drawn to the idea or how I could ever do it, but I just felt I could."

Paul didn't keep the secret from Tori for long though—he didn't even know why he was keeping it to himself anyhow.

When he told her, she immediately wanted to do it as well. There was something thrilling about this adventure that instantaneously excited them both. Neither of them still can put a finger on it now, other than that from the moment they heard they could row across the Atlantic Ocean, they wanted to do it.

How do we decide to do hard things, to become passionate about them, to build our fire?

For novice adventurers Paul and Tori, making the decision to row across the Atlantic Ocean was an easy one: they had the interest in doing it the moment they heard about it. The biggest hurdle they would face was maintaining their interest through the myriad of difficulties they would inevitably encounter in striving for that goal. In their book *Crossing the Swell: An Atlantic Journey by Rowboat*,[4] both Paul and Tori describe the decision process to undertake the challenge as a switch being flipped. They were immediately struck by the idea and the choice was easy. But the capacity to stay interested and committed to the idea, to eventually become passionate about it, was where the real challenge lay and where they demonstrated grit.

Like many adventurers, an idea to do something extraordinary starts as an attraction, a spark of interest, the allure of the unknown. For Paul it first happened with an idea to ride a bicycle across Australia. Paul had taken a year off from school to travel the world and was heading to Australia from New Zealand at the time. He was reading a copy of Lance Armstrong's *It's Not About the Bike*, several years before the celebrated cyclist was outed as a cheat, and he was struck by Armstrong's profoundly inspiring story of nearly dying from cancer, struggling through a gruelling recovery, and ultimately overcoming it and going on to win one of the toughest sporting challenges in the world, the Tour de France. "After reading the book," says Paul "I had an overwhelming urge to take on a big challenge myself."

Tori was in Australia at the same time Paul had arrived to undertake his bike ride. They didn't know one another at the time. She happened upon a flyer Paul had posted in a Melbourne youth hostel looking for someone to act as his support driver on his journey. Paul's posting caught her attention immediately. *"See Australia for free!"* the flyer said. *"Drive a support car for an Irish cyclist from Perth to Sydney and raise money for charity!"*

"It was as though this notice had been written for me," exclaimed Tori. "It was perfect for me. I had no money, so free travel was perfect, and the charity side was inspirational."

Paul had been captivated by the idea to cycle across Australia right away and acted on it as quickly. Tori was equally enthusiastic about helping him on his journey and jumped at it too. Just like with their row across the Atlantic, the interest in undertaking the adventure, be it riding or supporting, was instantaneous for both of them. It appealed to each of them at a visceral level. The kindling of their idea was ignited with the first match, but where Paul and Tori each displayed their immense capacity for grit was by stoking this interest into a fiery passion that would ultimately never burn out.

In her book, Duckworth states that many of us quit what we start far too early and far too often.[5] She makes it very clear that building a passion for something starts with a spark of interest just like Paul and Tori displayed on their adventures, but the capacity to stay with that interest, to move beyond the initial enthusiasm for it, beyond the initial honeymoon period, is how we build passion and purpose, and how we grow grit.

Building that fire requires intent. It requires deliberately investing time and effort into an interest, building knowledge and skill around that interest, growing it into something bigger, and developing it into a passion. There's little surprise that Duckworth's findings show that people perform better and are far more satisfied with their jobs when they do something that they are passionate about.

Simply put, to achieve a passion you need to work for it; interest will take you only so far. Anyone who has fallen in love understands this. The honeymoon period where the person you have fallen for can do no wrong does eventually wane, and when it does, you're left with a choice to make. For those who are committed and choose to stick with the relationship, nurturing it and developing it from an interest into a passion, they discover love. For those who don't, they discover heartbreak. The analogy here to a relationship is apt. By spending time deliberately improving something you enjoy—be it an idea, a pursuit, or a relationship—you'll continue enjoying it as you improve, and you will develop a passion for it over time.

In the sports and adventure world, this kind of deliberate practice directly increases grit. Grit is naturally adaptive in sport[6] due to number of hours required to develop sport-specific skills and the consistent time and effort that is required to improve fitness level and capability. This is something both Paul and Tori understand well as adventurers, but the concept neatly carries over to the business world as well. Engaging in sports outside of work can actually build additional levels of grit in the workplace. There is a positive association between the cognitive skills and grit gained through sport and its direct application in building perseverance at work for difficult, long-term tasks.

Michelle is the head of Product Policy for a large global technology company, and she understands the connection between sports outside of work and grit because she lives it. Michelle's career has taken her all over the place, both literally and figuratively. She has worked as a consultant, as a journalist, and as a key player in a global social impact venture, and now she works as a senior executive in the technology sector. Her diverse pursuits have taken her to every corner of the globe, and if there's one consistency to Michelle's life journey, it is its inconsistency. But through all her career transitions and global moves there's been one constant all along, Michelle's deep dedication to running. She's been a runner her entire life.

"There's definitely carryover between running and my work," she says. "The discipline, the breaking up of difficult challenges into manageable goals, persistence. Running helps me with all of those. It's made me more persistent and grittier in the face of challenge. I have had quite a few pivots in my career and it's helped."

Just recently we had an opportunity to speak with Michelle and she was seven months pregnant with her second child at the time. She wobbled into our conversation at her company's cafeteria wearing a plastic boot cast on her foot. "I landed wrong while running on a trail over at Castle Rock," she explained sheepishly. "It's my first running injury. I've been lucky, but I'm a bit sidelined. So now I'm on my outdoor elliptical bike. It's not the same, but it's still helping me get what I need." Her dedication to her pursuit is obvious.

"I'm a natural introvert, but in my job I spend most of my day with people. I need those runs to synthesize what happens during the day as well to reenergize and think. It's about making time for it, seeing it as a priority and what it can do for you versus a chore that must be done."

Although not a professional athlete, Michelle is sponsored, most recently running with the Oiselle team, a company that produces running apparel for women. "Running is actually a team sport, or it can be," she says. "When I run with other people, I get pushed to be better. It motivates me to chase those who are just a little bit faster than me." Michelle is well supported by her team, but also by her family. She's often joined on her runs and races by an enthusiastic cheering section, including her husband, two-year-old daughter, parents, and sister. Having this support network has allowed Michelle to run farther, longer, and faster than she probably would have otherwise.

"Funny enough," says Michelle, "I also use [running] to stoke my curiosity. When I'm traveling for work or even exploring locally, I use running as a way to see new things and explore. That definitely translates over to work and maintaining my sense of curiosity to find new projects or see new ideas in my work."

Running is both a physically and mentally rewarding activity that requires tremendous amounts of discipline and perseverance to remain committed to over the long term. It's been the one constant for Michelle, and through it she has increased her capacity to be disciplined, motivated, and persistent. Her deliberate practice of running has increased her overall grit in all aspects of her life: as a mother and wife, as a friend and colleague, and as a committed business professional.

Building your fire at work sometimes isn't as obvious. Amy is a sales enablement leader at a large company in Silicon Valley. For the past few years, one of her many responsibilities involves planning and running an annual sales learning event as part of the sales kickoff meeting for her company. Her organization brings together all its 8,000 salespeople for a multiday experience to review accomplishments, to reward achievements, and to share strategy for the upcoming year. These massive yearly gatherings require months and months of planning and coordination across the entire company. Amy is in the thick of it all, managing demands, timelines, and budgets with the expectations of her changing constantly. It's taxing, long-term work characterized by a roller-coaster ride of problem solving and personal sacrifice that Amy faces down year after year.

Perhaps many of us don't realize that a role in sales enablement could be a "dream job"; in fact, many of us might not even know what that work entails. But for Amy, this is where she has built her fire. "I've found I am really passionate about enabling others to be successful," she says. "I knew I could drive success and do a good job, so I stick with those hard, long-term projects. You do the hard stuff, you persevere, you learn from it, and it becomes part of your broader life story and gives you skills to use outside of work."

For Amy, building her fire was all about finding passion in the foundation of her work. She saw the opportunity to enable others to be successful and realized quickly it was something she was passionate about. She persevered through all the challenges she faced and now has become an integral member of her organization who is consistently recognized for contributing to the success of the sales team.

The Power of Perseverance

Often when we take on a new commitment, like when we get a promotion or take on a meatier role at work, we don't give much thought on how we will manage and succeed in that role over the long term. In the fast-moving modern business world, many corporations focus simply on the quarterly result, leaving employees little time to think about building personal sustainability over the long haul. The runways for most businesses are three months long at most, and at the end of that period, the clock resets with the new quarter, ticking through to the end of the year, at which point the whole feverish cycle begins again. This harried process, so commonplace in business these days, quickly leads to burnout. How can you, as an individual, build your own long-term sustainability and grit to handle these intense cycles?

Imagine that you've taken on a new role with increased responsibilities. You're excited about the new challenge and you look forward to what's ahead, but like with most new positions, you are a little uncertain about what lies in wait. You engage in a little "fake it till you make it" as you deal with parts of the job you're less familiar with, but you don't have an overall long-term plan for sustainability as you move forward. Let's take a lesson from Paul and Tori's playbook on how you might get there.

For the year before their Atlantic Ocean row, Paul and Tori prepared extensively. They knew the journey they'd be embarking on was going to push them to their limits physically, mentally, and emotionally, but they also knew, as a young couple, that their relationship was going to be tested as well. Their preparations took on a measure of commitment that many of us would struggle to replicate. On top of their full-time jobs, which monopolized the bulk of their daytime hours, the two intrepid adventurers followed a rigorous physical training regime that consisted of both morning and evening workouts throughout the week. And it didn't stop there. Paul and Tori needed to cover the significant cost of the expedition to make their adventure a reality, and this meant finding sponsors. So after a morning workout, a full day on the job, and a strenuous workout in the evening, Paul and Tori would spend their nights crafting sponsorship proposals. In an excerpt from *Crossing the Swell: An Atlantic Journey by Rowboat*, Paul describes his and Tori's struggles:

> Frequently, while driving home from work on a Friday evening, I would look out my window with envy at the crowds of people, both young and old, smiling, laughing and chatting over a few pints at the pub after a hard week's work. It may sound silly, but these were difficult moments for me. I had

worked myself to the bone throughout the week, trained hard and often woke up at my desk at home at three or four in the morning, having fallen asleep writing up sponsorship proposals or researching equipment. I would drag my weary body up the stairs to bed wondering what I had got myself into. But there would be no let-up, no time for recovery over the weekend; this was our busiest time. However, this was our choice; this was our life now; this was our daily grind.

And as we all know, Paul's lament is not exclusive to the adventurer. How often have you taken on a new task, a new role, or a new job and been faced with this dilemma? We all have. There will be those times when we question ourselves, just like Paul, and ask, "what have I got myself into?" But if we step back and rationalize that moment and answer the question with "this was our choice," then we will be much more likely to continue pursuing what we chose to pursue and persevere. Here lies the magic of grit. If what you're pursuing is really worth achieving, then it's going to require dedication and hard work to achieve it. Perseverance is not easy, it's never easy, and that's the point. Being gritty will get you there.

Paul and Tori knew full well what they had got themselves into and did everything in their power to mitigate the effects. They ate better, exercised more, and became more focused on their relationship with each other. The two became fastidious about their daily diet. "Our house was like a produce farm," says Tori, "We just couldn't afford to let our immune systems break down. We had so much ahead of us. Eating unhealthily affected our energy levels, and we couldn't let that happen. There was no way."

They ramped up their exercise volume and found to their surprise that the rigorous exercise wasn't draining their energy but stoking it. The science on the subject is definitive that routine exercise has a powerful capacity to reduce stress and increase resilience, but Paul and Tori hadn't planned on it—they just wanted to get super fit for their journey. The simple act of getting really fit was now paying unexpected dividends as the two adventurers were better able to cope with the stresses from everything else they were facing.

And, of course, Paul and Tori were very cognizant of their relationship and the stresses it would have to bear through this difficult time. But much like with their exercise routine, the two made a discovery. Their relationship, which was under stress, was the same relationship that was helping them navigate that stress. They found that the challenge of the planning ordeal was actually drawing them closer together and making them stronger. The support and motivation provided by each other for each other was allowing them to persevere through all the turmoil and was making them grittier. No matter what happened, they always had each other to turn to.

Building your capability to persevere for the long haul in the business world involves many of the same preparation routines Paul and Tori undertook. Understanding that your performance at work relies on a wider range of capabilities other than just knowing the technical components of your job is the first step. Unfortunately, most people focus on the knowledge and skills they need for their work performance over the short term without realizing that they need to build physical, emotional, and relationship capacity to perform over the long term. A balance in all these areas is an essential part of building grit.

We have clients from all over the world, and we're always struck by how many focus solely on their mental capacity at the expense of everything else—their health, their friends and family, or their emotional well-being. As human beings, we operate as a "networked system" and need to fuel and care for the other elements of our performance to operate at our best. Strong mental capacity is important, but equally important is our physical, emotional, and relationship capacity. Far too many business professionals log in 16-hour days fueled on poor food choices and caffeine, omitting exercise because of lack of time, only to expect to wind down with a dose of Chardonnay in the evenings.

Paul and Tori demonstrated clearly that by incorporating rigorous exercise into their schedules, by eating well, and by being mindful of each other's emotional well-being, they would perform at their best. They naturally balanced their mental, physical, emotional, and relationship capacities, and in many ways, by pure circumstance, they discovered the secret to building their aptitude for perserverence and grit. We can all learn from their discovery.

Were Paul and Tori more capable because of their preparation? Definitely. The year they spent building their robustness was critical to making them grittier on their journey. They dealt with their challenges leading up to the row by growing their grit, and this, in turn, helped them face challenges out on the Atlantic. Indeed, the more protracted a struggle is going to be, the more robust and tenacious in your mental, physical, emotional, and relationship strengths you will have to be.

Building Your Grit to Persevere

Building your own ability to persevere for the long term is another tool in your high-performance toolkit. Grit allows you to take a spark of interest and fan it into a much larger, brighter-burning flame. Here are three ways to build your grit for long-term performance:

1. **Rewrite your positive story.** Take your passion and create your positive story. You may decide to do something that seems well out of your comfort zone or capability. If you create a positive story about believing you can do the extraordinary, your chances of accomplishing that feat are much higher. Create a story that is positive and outcome-focused. Tell that positive story to others, and surround yourself with the people in your life who will believe in your capabilities.

2. **Fake it 'till you make it—build your perseverance.** Know that to build grit, you're going to be uncomfortable, and that is part of the learning process. However, with your positive story and belief, you can create smaller opportunities to build up your capabilities, increasing your confidence. Much like Jennifer's story we looked at earlier in the chapter, those small experiences, whether or not they are related to your work or outside of it, build capabilities to help you persevere. Recognize those moments when you discover something new, and congratulate yourself for being brave and bold enough to try. As Angela Duckworth says, "in the marathon of life, effort counts tremendously."[7]

3. **Control what you can.** Finally, realizing the importance of your internal locus of control is critical. Letting go of the things you can't control and focusing and preparing on what you can control is vital. Paul and Tori knew they could ready the boat, work on their physical conditioning, and be mentally prepared, but they could not control the ocean that they would face. They could stay positive in their capability and belief because of the fact they had managed and prepared the factors they could control, and that led to their ultimate success.

* * *

"For as long as I live, I will never forget that feeling when we saw land for the first time," says Paul. "Tori was rowing and I was standing in front of her, just outside the main cabin. My eyes suddenly opened wide, nearly peeling open my entire face. 'Land! Tori! I shouted. Land! There's land!' We both stood gazing out at a tiny part of the world we had been dreaming about for three months. We made it. It was one of those special moments in life that we all sometimes have, one we knew we would remember forever."[8]

February 22, 2006, after 84 days, 23 hours, and 12 minutes at sea, Paul Gleeson and Tori Holmes stepped ashore in Antigua, successfully rowing 4,700 kilometers across the Atlantic Ocean. An offhand question from a friend 18 months earlier was transformed into an insatiable yearning for both Paul and Tori, who then because of their unrelenting grit manifested their passion into action and persevered, ultimately allowing that flicker of an idea to became a life-changing reality. Without grit, Paul and Tori's seemingly preposterous dream of rowing an ocean with no rowing experience would never have become a reality.

"One thing I will say, and I don't think it's being arrogant," says Paul, "but I genuinely believe that if I really want to do something in life and work hard toward achieving it, then I can do it. Nothing can stop me if I truly want it."[9]

CHAPTER 3

Growth Mindset

Sitting Still Means Going Backward

Standing at the top of the world for the third time, Matt McFadyen was struck by an overwhelming sense of disbelief. He had made it to the North Pole again, grasping the arctic grail of polar exploration for a seemingly impossible third time. It was an astonishing effort, as impressive as it was implausible. More people have been to outer space than have traveled to the North Pole on foot, yet here he was. Matt was only 28 years old, and during his brief career as an adventurer, he had garnered international recognition as both an open ocean sailor and world-class polar explorer. This was a dream beyond measure for the young Australian, and he knew it.

"You see, mate, where I grew up, you didn't do this sort of thing. The guys I grew up with are salt of the earth kind of guys, you know, working class, a shovel by day, saddled up to the bar at night."

And it did not stop there. Just five years earlier, after a harrowing sailing expedition across the Southern Ocean to Antarctica and back, Matt had found the courage to stand up in front of an audience and share his story. The response had been extraordinary, and before he knew it, he had become a much sought-after public speaker delivering keynote presentations to thousands of people around the world. If you did not know any better, you would assume success was predestined for Matt, a simple exercise like rolling out a carpet in front of him. You would be wrong.

Matt grew up in a working-class neighborhood of Sydney, Australia, with a father who walked out on him and his family when he was six years old. "He gambled the house away, and then he just walked out. He left me, mom, and my brother with nothing," he says. "We had to live with my grandparents for eight years because Mom worked hard but couldn't afford her own place to live."

Matt completed his high school education, but eschewed higher learning, looking for something exciting. It was a scenario seemingly predestined for mediocrity: a young man from an underprivileged family with only a high school education looking for something bold and new.

Yet just over a decade later, Matt was standing at the North Pole as an internationally recognized explorer with a burgeoning career as a professional speaker. It was a far-fetched journey for someone with such a meager start, but here he was, achieving the seemingly impossible. How had he done it? How had he navigated a path to success so quickly? Was Matt simply just better than everyone else with natural talents that chartered his success or was there something else guiding his way?

Matt McFadyen at the Ninnis and Mertz Memorial Cross near Mawson's hut, Azimuth Hill, Antarctica

Courtesy of Matt McFadyen

What Is a Growth Mindset?

"The view you adopt for yourself profoundly affects the way you lead your life."[1] These words from the celebrated researcher on motivation and achievement Carol Dweck speak to how Matt McFadyen has accomplished all he has. Matt is an exemplar of having what Carol Dweck calls a growth mindset. In her seminal 2006 book, *Mindset*, Dweck describes how your approach and view of the world allows you to achieve more for yourself because of your belief in yourself and your capabilities. Matt McFadyen's mindset charted his course to success more likely than any other factor.

At the core of Dweck's *Mindset* and why it is so important for leaders is that it describes a new understanding of brain plasticity, the ability for our brains to continue to learn and grow, increasing and strengthening with experience and practice. This growth factor can help us achieve beyond our wildest dreams, and it is part of Matt's secret to success.

Our brains can often work against us. We are negatively wired for survival. Our brain defaults to latching on to negative outcomes as well as worst-case-scenarios as a survival mechanism that has helped us stay alive over thousands of years. Managing this predisposition to negativity can drastically improve our attitude and approach to any situation.

At its core, mindset is defined by two approaches: fixed and growth. A fixed mindset is a fixed definition on belief, challenges, capabilities, and interpretation of events. It is a somewhat fatalist view of the world and often has us in a victim mentality, essentially believing that what happens in the world just "is" and is predestined, instead of anything we can interpret differently or change. A growth mindset, however, unlocks an unshakable attitude, turning our experiences, beliefs, and skill development into useful information from which we can adapt and learn.

As humans, we do not display just a fixed or growth mindset but typically, depending on the context, something in between. Our natural response to situations, where we get feedback or face a challenge, is influenced by many factors, including how we have faced a similar challenge in the past, how we have been conditioned to receive feedback, and how internal self-talk has shaped our beliefs.

Looking for Opportunities to Grow

One of the first key elements to having a growth mindset is the effort you put into a situation. As Matt the plain-spoken Aussie explains, "Mate, I've busted my ass to get where I've gotten to in my life today, there's been no shortcuts. I've got to where I've got because of two things: I've been given great opportunities and I've taken those opportunities and I've run with them." No doubt, to become an adventurer of Matt's caliber requires incredibly hard work and a vision to see situations as learning opportunities. Matt demonstrated a growth mindset by embracing opportunity and challenge and not worrying on whether or not he would be thought of as silly or foolish in doing so. He never limited his aspirations because of his humble beginnings.

It all began for Matt at the age of fifteen, when he asked his mom to buy him a learn-to-sail course for Christmas and was met with a look of disbelief. "You see, my dad, who I didn't really know at all, was a sailor," explains Matt. "He was a really good sailor and he grew up sailing all his life. My mom was kind of floored when I told her that I wanted to learn how to sail, just like him."

Sailing is what he wanted to do and his mother supported him. When Matt headed out on the water, he discovered a taste for adventure that changed his life forever. It was during his second time sailing on the water, coming out of a bay into Sydney Harbor with a 20-knot wind at his back, that it all clicked. "I remember the boat keeling over and just powering on and falling in love with it all instantly." And before he knew it, Matt began to orchestrate his life around his newfound passion and pursued it relentlessly, taking every opportunity to sail.

"I used to take two trains and then ride my skateboard into the yacht club every Sunday morning by 7:00 a.m. just to try to pick up spots on boats when crew members didn't show up," says Matt. "I just wanted to get on board a boat any way I could." Matt focused on learning as much as he could about sailing and working hard to practice his skills. He knew that with discipline and focus it would help him improve over time.

His passion did not go unnoticed by the local sailing community, and before long he began to pick up more permanent roles as a crew member on boats. He started to dabble in yacht racing during the summer and winter months in Sydney, but in his mind, it was just a means to an end. "I had no intention of becoming a professional racer," he says. "I remember I'd always sail past Sydney Head, the entrance to Sydney Harbor, and look out past it and think there's a huge ocean out there. I always dreamed about sailing something bigger, about sailing around the world."

When it comes to seeking out opportunities to grow, we can be our own worst enemies, with the fear of the unknown often holding us back. In Matt's case, he chased after opportunities to learn sailing, but when it came to a job shift and learning to be a business facilitator, that transition was more difficult. Matt often would struggle with realizing the value he could add in enhancing a team's collaboration, because he didn't have extensive business experience or education. He had to surmount that hurdle and be open to the possibility that stories about teamwork and leadership from his adventures could provide great value. Moving past that uncertainty is key. And for many of us, when a new role or job opportunity arises, we can be hesitant to take it on. According to Rachel Cardero and Andrea Derler, of the NeuroLeadership Institute, "When we feel highly uncertain, our attention narrows and our cognitive function suffers."[2] This narrowing of focus can be helpful in some fight-or-flight situations but is a huge detriment when we are trying to expand our horizons and learn something new. To grow we need to identify and recognize this fear and then take steps to overcome it. By acknowledging this fear as part of our natural, biological reaction to uncertainty, we can better set it aside and move forward into that new opportunity.

Learning from Feedback

As Matt's passion for adventure grew, so did his focus on open-ocean sailing. "I started following around-the-world sailors," he says, "and I read an article about Tony Mowbray who was 100 days into a 181-day solo circumnavigation of the planet. He listed a website at the end of the article, and that night, I sent him an email, and much to my surprise within 24 hours he emailed me back from the Southern Ocean." Tony had been alone on his journey and was craving conversation. Matt's email came at the perfect moment. "He told me later he would have talked to anyone at that point," says Matt. "Even some snotty-nosed kid from back home in Australia."

Looking back, this was the first time Matt consciously reached out to seek advice from someone who exemplified the capabilities he wanted to build. Just like with his embracing of opportunity, it was strongly indicative of Matt's growth mindset. Tony Mowbray would prove to be the first in a long line of people over the coming years who would help guide Matt and give him the honest feedback he needed. And to be clear, the honest feedback he needed was not always the feedback Matt wanted to hear.

Honest feedback can often be a hard pill to swallow and being willing to accept feedback, particularly critical feedback, is as important as finding that valuable source in the first place. Matt wanted to improve and to do so opened himself up to input, no matter how difficult and painful it might be to hear it. Through his affable nature he built a network of people who would help transform his performance. By leaning in to the discomfort of feedback, and seeing it as a building block rather than a personal affront, Matt was able to use it as a means to address his shortcomings and successfully grow.

What started out as a simple gesture by Matt in reaching out to Tony Mowbray grew into a fast friendship that two years later would see Matt lining up with Tony and three other sailors to take on a voyage to Antarctica across the Southern Ocean, one of the most infamous bodies of water on the planet. The 54-day journey at sea would change his life forever.

The Southern Ocean is notorious for the frequency and ferociousness of its storms. High winds, generated by the strong pressure gradients between the subtropical high-pressure belt and the sub-Antarctic trough, race around the continent of Antarctica unabated, producing a seascape described by those who know as the "roaring forties" and "furious fifties" at each of the 40th and 50th parallels. Matt and his team, well aware of what they were getting into, anticipated very rough weather and violent winds on their journey. Unfortunately for them, the Southern Ocean had much more in store.

As fate would have it, two colossal storms marauding around the mid-latitudes of the Southern Ocean joined forces to become a cyclone of legendary size and ferocity. The team of five, who at the time were on their return leg back from Antarctica, realized they were sailing right across the storm's path. The cyclone was too fast moving to avoid, and before they knew it, they were engulfed in a tempest of biblical proportions, fighting for their lives.

The team's 43-foot yacht was no match for the storm, and when huge breaking waves began to sweep over the bow, their world was literally turned upside down. Matt was alone on deck when the boat was hit broadside by a gigantic wave and rolled. "It was a 50-footer with the upper 20 feet curling, breaking, and frothing," recalls Matt. "All I remember was . . . boom! . . . and suddenly, I'm underwater with the boat above me. I was desperate for air and I was clambering to undo my emergency tether line that attached me to the boat. I couldn't breathe. I needed to get air. I needed to unclip the line. I needed to get air!" As Matt fumbled with his clip, the boat was hit by another wave and rolled back upright again, leaving him right back where he started from on deck, stunned but otherwise uninjured. It only dawned on him then that if had he succeeded in unclipping his tether line moments earlier, he would still be in the ocean now, far away from the boat and lost at sea.

The cyclone-strength storm would rage unabated for days, with the sailing team expecting the worst every time a wave thundered into the hull. It got so bad at one point that the team said their good-byes and waited on the inevitable to come. Luckily, it never did.

That death-defying experience affected Matt for life, and it was a catalyst for him to look for something else. "I became petrified of the ocean after that experience," explains Matt, "As scary as that adventure was, it did give me a very different outlook on life. It's cliché, but I realized life can be taken away from you in a blink of an eye. I had a choice to make. I could have gone, 'OK, that's it. It was a great experience and that's enough for me,' but instead I thought I have only one life and I will keep pursuing my passion of adventure. I will just do it differently."

"Confronting failure and learning from mistakes is an essential part of the process of developing a growth mindset," according to Ian Johnston in his research published in the article "Creating a Growth Mindset" in *Strategic HR Review*.[3] Accepting failure as an integral part of the learning process is a fundamental tenet of growth mindset and can help us be better leaders and better human beings. After Matt's ordeal on the Southern Ocean, he was faced with an important decision to make in his adventuring career: continue or quit. Flipping from a fixed mindset to a growth mindset is not an easy one and requires deep and reflective learning through an iterative process of adjustment and improvement. Recognition of what you learn from a challenge and understanding that the lessons you learn are often emotional in nature are important parts of being authentic in your growth mindset. Matt's eagerness to continue adventuring in a different milieu demonstrates his desire for continued opportunity to grow in the face of failure.

Believe in Your Capacity to Grow

After the storm passed, Matt and his team had a week more of sailing to make it back to harbor in Australia. Matt set about distracting himself from his surroundings in any way he could, still in a state of shock after his near-death experience. "I read anything and everything that was on the boat," he explains. "And I found an article in a *National Geographic* magazine about the first Australian team to ski to the North Pole. I didn't even know polar adventure existed but it intrigued me. I suppose the beauty of youth, or naiveté, is that I found the guide's name, Eric Philips, and I literally called him up when I got back to shore and said to him, 'I want to go to the North Pole. Can you help me?'" In just 18 months after that first conversation, Matt was skiing atop the frozen surface of the Arctic Ocean making his way to the North Pole.

Here is the thing about Matt: he is unafraid to ask for help and unafraid of showing himself as being unintelligent, as so many people with fixed mindsets are scared to do. This is a core element of having a growth mindset. As Carol Dweck explicitly points out in her article "Mindsets and Human Nature," "Much research has shown that when people hold a fixed mindset about their own traits, such as their intelligence, they tend to avoid challenges for fear of showing themselves to be unintelligent."[4] At work, that translates to us not raising our hand in a meeting for fear of looking stupid. It is those times when we don't put ourselves forward for a promotion or to lead a project because we are worried we aren't 100 percent qualified for all aspects of the job. Our fear of failure and looking unintelligent can prevent us from garnering those true moments of growth. Matt could not have been more out of his element, a sun-loving Australian sailor thinking of heading to the North Pole, but he had a belief in himself that he could work hard and accomplish this goal, using the feedback from an expert, persisting when things got difficult, and believing the quest would be a growth opportunity.

All of us will eventually be faced with a similar "out of your element" challenge. According to one study by McKinsey

Global Institute, up to 375 million workers globally will need to change roles or learn dramatically new skills by 2030. The world is changing rapidly and automation will have a far-reaching impact. The idea that each of us could make such a pivot to learn new skills will be a challenge not only for individuals but for companies and even entire countries. Retraining yourself and believing that you can create a new chapter will be critical for those individuals needing to make career changes. No longer can we expect to have one key role in a domain for an entire career.

Important to note, over the past few years *growth mindset* has become a ubiquitous buzzword in business circles, and clarifying what it *isn't* is just as important as understanding what it is. Simple definitions associating growth mindset with a "growth of your business," "growing an organization," or even the "limitlessness of unbounded growth" are misguided and inaccurate. At its most fundamental level, growth mindset starts with the individual—with the belief you can learn and grow by working hard, failing, and trying again—and then is carried forward through the business.

Spreading a growth mindset at the organizational level requires a deep shift in the core belief that all individuals at a company can transform and change to face new challenges. This belief must start at the CEO level and permeate down through the entire leadership structure of the company. One significant and current example of growth mindset organization-wide is Microsoft in its efforts to regain its relevance.[5] It is a remarkable story of ongoing transformation, spearheaded by CEO Satya Nadella and his own belief in himself, his company, and the concept of instilling growth mindset across every person in the company.

In February 2014, Nadella took over the helm at a company known for internal infighting, lackluster products, and tanking stock prices. The market had shifted into mobile, and

Microsoft was struggling to compete. Within the organization, stack ranking fostered an environment of deep political games and backstabbing, with many resting on their laurels surmising the company to be too big to fail.

Nadella was eight months into his tenure when he gave a keynote at the Grace Hopper Celebration of Women in Computing, an annual tech industry event for women. During the Q&A at the end, computer scientist and former Microsoft board member Dr. Maria Klawe asked Nadella his advice for women seeking a pay raise who may be too apprehensive to ask. Nadella suggested that a woman should be patient and that "knowing and having faith that the system will actually give you the right raises as you go along." His answer sparked outrage, his comments went viral, and many openly questioned his commitment to diversity. It was a critical moment for Nadella as a leader. Instead of letting the storm blow over, he decided to meet it head-on.

During this tumultuous time, Nadella's wife, Anupama, shared a copy of Carol Dweck's book *Mindset* with him, and it spurred a deep reflection on the challenges he was facing as a leader. "I was determined to use the incident to demonstrate what a growth mindset looks like under pressure," he said.[6]

Starting with himself, Nadella transitioned the mindset of everyone in the company and challenged them to believe they could overcome any constraint or challenge. He owned up to his public mistake and demonstrated that he was going to learn and grow from it. As objectively as possible, he looked at his own biases and encouraged his executive leadership team to do the same. It was a transformative exercise for Nadella, and because of it, he now focuses on progress and the striving for improvement rather than fixed traits like talent.

Over the last five years, Microsoft's transformation has been clear and well-documented. Its share price is at an all-time high, and the company is regaining its reputation for innovation, becoming a real competitor in the market again. The effort continues today, as developing growth mindset is a continuous journey. A growth mindset demands learning and evolution and is never an easy process. But with using it comes revitalization and success both at the individual and organization levels, as clearly demonstrated by Nadella.

Take a Risk + Put in the Effort

Looking down at his GPS, Matt realized he was standing on the roof of the world, 90-degrees north: the North Pole. It was a fleeting moment as the ice beneath him, just an ephemeral frozen skin on the Arctic Ocean, drifted off the 90-degree mark, and he began to look for it again. It was a poignant reminder to the young adventurer that sitting still meant going backward. But Matt was overjoyed. He had made it. He had become the youngest Australian to ever reach the North Pole. It was just a year and a half earlier that he had finished his perilous sailing expedition to Antarctica, and over that short period of time, he transformed himself into a world-class polar explorer.

Matt had undertaken the North Pole expedition with polar guide Eric Philips, who he had reached out to at the end of his sailing expedition, and his perseverance and willingness to learn had so impressed Philips that shortly after their return home to Australia, he asked Matt to join him on a North Pole expedition the following year as a guide.

"Literally 12 months later to the day I stood at the North Pole again," says Matt. "I was an assistant guide on a team of eight. It was the same expedition but completely different in terms of the responsibilities I had. I took more pleasure out of that trip because I was able to help the first Australian woman in history to get the North Pole." Matt had two close friends from high school join him on the trip as well, and he proved to himself how quickly and effectively he could transform himself if he really wanted to. "There were much deeper takeaways on this journey," he says. "I realized with a little risk and a lot of effort I could do amazing things!"

Matt McFadyen celebrating his arrival at the North Pole   *Courtesy of Matt McFadyen*

After his second expedition to the North Pole, Matt began to focus more and more on his speaking career. "I put a lot of time into it," he says. "It's a tough nut to crack, and I realized I was good at it. I hadn't planned to go back (to the North Pole) a third time, but when the opportunity came up, I jumped at it realizing it was an opportunity to continue to grow my skills as an adventurer and as a leader." The opportunity came when Matt was working with PricewaterhouseCoopers (PwC) as a speaker on a global road show and was sitting in an airport lounge in Adelaide, South Australia, with the CEO, Tony Harrington. Tony looked down from his newspaper and asked Matt: "Have you ever thought about going to the North Pole again?"

"Before I had time to answer with 'absolutely no intention whatsoever,'" says Matt jokingly, "Tony replied with 'I've spoken to the board of directors and we want to sponsor your trip.' Trying to find money is hard but when someone throws it at you, I said, 'Absolutely, Tony, I was just planning my next expedition to go back!'"

Matt had now begun to operate in the corporate environment and was very self-conscious of his age and lack of education. "I was 27 at the time, sitting in boardrooms with managing directors and the CEO of one the biggest consulting companies in the world," he says. "Here I was with no real corporate experience and felt like I was sort of winging it."

Matt was tasked to be an ambassador for PwC and was given three very clear objectives to deliver upon. It was by striving for these objectives that he began to see how leadership learning from the adventure world informed business behavior.

The first of his three objectives was to help differentiate PwC in the green marketplace. The company had created a new arm of their business called Climate Change and Sustainability Services, and they wanted to become a market leader in the field. The senior partner and leader of this new business wanted to experience an environment that had become the "canary in the coal mine" for climate change, and where better to see those changes firsthand than at the North Pole. It was Matt's job to get him there.

His second objective was to help use this North Pole expedition to increase PwC's top talent pool. Market research had indicated that top graduates were now looking for more than a financially successful company to work for; they were also looking for companies with deep and impactful global purpose. Matt's sponsored expedition would be a symbol of this.

The third objective was to increase employee engagement scores and create a buzz in the firm through blogs, multimedia presentations, and an inspirational internal intranet site. "They had huge murals in their head offices and one of them was me in my polar kit," says Matt with a laugh. He understood the need to make this journey compelling.

"The trip itself was tough," he continues. "It was a really tough and cold season. We went early in the season because of the amount of open water right at the back end of winter. Ben, the partner from PwC, was used to the finer things in life and more luxurious travel. Here I am at 27 telling him what to do, a man in his early forties. He said to me out on the ice, 'I'm used to telling people what to do. I'm struggling with you telling me what to do,' but I had to in order to keep him safe."

Matt's pivot on his third expedition, incorporating the challenge of tying his expedition to specific business objectives, challenged him deeply. As an experienced polar explorer at this point, he understood what was needed from a planning, preparation, and physical point of view to be successful on the ice. But this third journey to the pole required him to grow his leadership capabilities and learn how to communicate, motivate, and inspire someone else to tackle the challenge of reaching the North Pole and teach them the skills he had already mastered. Much like a subject matter expert who is thrust into a managerial role with people management responsibilities, Matt had to grow his leadership capabilities quickly. He learned through the experience and succeeded because he was willing to take a chance and make the effort. Matt helped Ben successfully set foot on the North Pole, and he made it there himself for the third time. "I nailed all three of the objectives as well," he says. "Eleven years later and this journey provided the building blocks for where I am today." And where Matt is today is squarely in the corporate world. He again has successfully transformed himself by learning and growing to become something he never dreamed of.

On this third journey, Matt discovered that he enjoyed learning to be a leader, and through his experience with PwC, he realized he could connect the leadership lessons learned from the adventure world back to business. Matt made the shift from professional adventurer into leadership facilitator with a consulting company called The AIP Group (in full disclosure, the same consulting company the authors of this book work with), perhaps one of his most daunting challenges yet.

Over the course of the next 11 years, Matt hit the pause button on his adventures to learn the ropes of business, once again putting his growth mindset to the test. Working as a lead facilitator, Matt led workshops on leadership development skills and shared his stories from the adventure world. His interaction with business leaders from some of the top Fortune 500 companies was perhaps Matt's most daunting challenge, but it was also his greatest opportunity for growth. At first, Matt relied on just telling compelling adventure stories in these business sessions, but soon realized he wanted to work harder to make connections and dive deeper into equipping people and teams with practical skills. He knew he needed to learn a different language, a business language, to provide relevance beyond just a novel story of adventure.

Not only did he want to inspire people, he wanted them to walk away making deeper, stronger connections. But Matt had to do this for himself before he could help others. So he sought out feedback from his colleagues and peers, accepting difficult and constructive input openly, and humbly realized that he had a long road ahead if he was going to be a credible authority. He gradually learned how businesses worked by watching, listening, and asking questions and eventually overcame his own concern about feeling uneducated. Business concepts did not come naturally to him, and he depended heavily on his team for their feedback, input, and advice. Over time, Matt developed and grew his knowledge and understanding, and today continues to evolve his facilitating skills and understanding of business.

Matt McFadyen skiing across a lead, or gap, in the sea ice on his way to the North Pole
Courtesy of Matt McFadyen

Being smart and talented is not something you are given, but something you earn. Through hard effort, learning, and developing a growth mindset, we're able to transform ourselves. If you really want to get good at something and you believe in your own neuroplasticity through sustained effort to get good at it, then you will. This is the fundamental tenet of having a growth mindset. We are all capable of achieving the extraordinary if we are willing to risk a little and work a lot.

How to Build Your Growth Mindset

Taking a page from Matt's book on continuing to look for opportunities to grow, getting feedback, and facing setbacks, here are the three key lessons we can learn from him:

1. **Look for opportunities.** Often the fear of the unknown or the fear of looking foolish stops us from taking opportunities that will allow us to grow and succeed. Matt's humble background never stopped him from looking forward and dreaming of opportunities for himself. It's only when we can cast off our fears and seek out those unique opportunities that we will experience learning and growth and achieve our greatest potential.

2. **Seek and learn from feedback.** In the business world, feedback is often seen as a loaded gun, with the phrase "can I give you some feedback" tying our stomach in knots and causing us anxiety. But by looking at feedback differently, as psychologist Carol Dweck suggests, and seeing it as a building block for growth and a welcome opportunity to get better, you can shed the emotional taxation that feedback creates. At the end of the day, if someone cares enough to share constructive criticism with you (likely as challenging for them to share as for you to hear), they're doing it to help you and because they care about your growth. Finding trusted advisors who will give you honest feedback on your performance and then treating this feedback as an opportunity to improve is key to building a growth mindset.

3. **Take risks and work hard.** Matt's courage to take risks and reach out, first to Tony Mowbray, then to Eric Philips, shows what can happen to an ordinary guy who

takes a chance. His ensuing expeditions were fraught with peril and required enormous amounts of hard work, but Matt's capacity to see past the challenge and undertake them anyway speaks to both his success and his growth mindset.

* * *

In addition to those three lessons, there is an important additional lesson from Matt on how to persist in the face of setbacks.

The following is an event Matt has recently faced and again exemplifies his growth mindset. The story is shared through the voice of author Amy Posey, who experienced it firsthand, and we thank Matt for being open enough to share it with us.

Growth mindset allows you to cope with the depression that sometimes accompanies setbacks. Matt faced his biggest setback in July 2018.

Toothbrush in hand, I looked down at my phone an early and warm July Saturday morning. It was strange to see Matt calling so early on a weekend. A week earlier, Matt had mentioned that he went to the doctor because he and his wife, Meg, noticed a strange mark on his back. Jokingly, I asked him why he was spending so much time topless at work, and we had both laughed it off. But I heard the concern in his voice as well as the hope that it was nothing. Ever the optimist, Matt is not one to look at the dark side of life, and this was no different.

But the phone call I received that Saturday morning was different. My stomach tightened and a light wave of nausea went through me as I heard his voice on the other end. I knew right away that things were going to be different, no matter what he was about to tell me. I could tell from his first exhale that it was bad news. And it was indeed bad news. Matt's doctor called to let him know that he had developed a malignant melanoma on his back. He had stage 2 skin cancer, and he needed surgery to remove it immediately. There was a high potential for it to have already spread to his lymph nodes. Through tears and the nervous fear only a terrifying diagnosis can give you, we talked through what was going to happen and what he needed to do. Mostly, though, we cried and were scared together as friends and colleagues.

"What am I going to tell people?" he said to me over the phone, his voice shaky and anxious. "What if it's spread? What if it's really bad?" A lot of the natural what-if questions came out, and I did all I could do, which was plan for what we actually did know and could do. Matt had cancer and he had to have surgery. We would tell only those who needed to know, and we would figure out how to cover his workload and give him time off and support.

For Matt, it was a moment of extreme setback—a moment to dig deep, once again, into his growth mindset toolkit. Truth be told, it was very hard to find those tools in that moment of despair. How do you approach a serious skin cancer diagnosis with a growth mindset?

But Matt had faced another serious health issue before and found the courage to work through it. After his third journey to the North Pole he had developed a debilitating back injury from countless days of dragging a 200-pound sled. Matt was in extreme pain and began to struggle with even the most basic daily routines. He eschewed the idea of surgery, petrified it would end his adventuring career, and he began to heed the advice of misinformed friends who said that "surgery wouldn't fix the problem" and that he was "too young for such a bad back." His pain worsened and so did his quality of life. He began to depend on alcohol and painkillers to ease the pain. Finally one day, lying immobile on his living room floor, he faced the reality of his situation. He faced his fear, heeded his doctor's advice, and underwent surgery. In a short time he was back to his old self. He had learned not to let fear inhibit his actions, and it was a learning he'd need to use again.

From the outset of his cancer diagnosis, Matt focused on the actions he could take rather than dwelling on the what-ifs. He stepped away from an overwhelming sense of hopelessness and instead focused on making a game plane. As a core member of a small team and the face of a small business, he knew he would be sorely missed. He crafted a story to tell clients and talked to the team about taking time off to focus on himself, his health, and his recovery. By doing this, he was able to make some jokes, as many Australians do, and try to keep as upbeat as best he could. The team reinforced his optimism and talked to him about the opportunity to continue growing, and eventually telling this exact story on applying a growth mindset to the deepest and most difficult setbacks. Even in his darkest moment, Matt knew there would be a lesson to learn.

We are thrilled to share that surgery and recovery went smoothly for Matt and he's fully on the mend. He weathered this setback in life by applying a growth mindset, by reaching out to friends and colleagues for support, by recognizing early on in his battle that countless people have successfully navigated such a diagnosis, and by doing everything he could to stay upbeat and in a positive headspace through the taxing ordeal. Matt showed up and with a growth mindset he did what he had to do, and because of it, he is now happy, healthy, and a stronger person for it.

CHAPTER 4

Purpose

Finding Your Spark

t was a gloomy, gray January morning in London, England, as Roz Savage dashed toward the railway station. It had been raining all night, and a shroud of cold mist from the road, kicked up by passing cars and buses, enveloped her as she raced to make her 7:11 a.m. train. Roz stopped briefly at the newsstand to grab a morning paper, something she did every morning, and then joined the throngs making their daily commute into the city. It was a day much like every other day for her, a day she had experienced many times over the last 11 years. But today was different—today, her life would change forever.

"The 7:11 train arrived and my husband and I got on," she says. "We sat down in our usual seats and opened our newspapers. But I was distracted . . . what was wrong with me today?"

Something had been eating away at Roz, and she couldn't explain it. It was an intuition, a feeling, an unexplained angst that something was missing in her life, and it was confusing her. She was following her life's plan to a tee, doing everything she was supposed to be doing to make her happy. She had attended prestigious Oxford University and upon graduation immediately began a promising career in business as a management consultant. For the next 11 years, she steadily climbed the corporate ladder, attaining her goals and reaching her milestones, but it hadn't felt right. Along the way, Roz married a highly intelligent, charismatic man and with him found financial security and material comfort. The norms of society had suggested that moving forward like this was the means to finding happiness, so she kept moving forward, doing what she felt she should regardless of the fact that it felt wrong. "I wasn't thriving," she says, "And now I can see it's because work meant nothing to me. But at the time, it was a source of self-doubt and plummeting self-esteem. No matter how things looked on paper, I felt deep inside something wasn't right."

Her feeling of malaise had been eating away at her for some time, but today, in the overcrowded train to work, she felt dissatisfaction like never before. Looking around her train car, she recognized many of the commuters seated near her, the daily travelers, like herself, doing what they do, heads buried in their papers blocking out the world around them. One middle-aged man caught her attention. "He was of indeterminate age, probably about 50 but maybe not as old as he looked," she explains. He was someone she'd seen many times before, neatly dressed in a suit and raincoat with his collar done up just a little too tight. He had a drinker's nose and a vacant stare, his ruddy complexion adding a flush of anxiety to an otherwise blank facade of resignation. "He looked as if every ounce of youthful energy, every vestige of enthusiasm for life, every iota of idealism had been sucked out of him," she says.

The man turned the page of his newspaper and the obituary section came into view. Columns of small black-and-white photos, each with a short paragraph beneath them, marched across the paper. These human lives distilled into headshots and a smattering of words, a person's very essence, their final outcome, revealed for everyone to see. The reality jolted Roz. "What would people say about me when I died?" she thought. "Would I be worth an obituary? Or would I just pass away unnoticed, my life as fleeting and insignificant as a mayfly's? Would I end up like the man sitting opposite me, merely existing, rather than living?"

The reason for her recent uneasiness was now becoming clearer. "I had been living a conventional life, doing what I thought I was supposed to do, conforming to the norm and following the crowd," she says. "Now that mask had cracked, and for a moment I glimpsed what might be. Or indeed, who might be. Could there really be a more interesting and independent person behind this mask, waiting to emerge into the light?"

Throughout the day, Roz couldn't shake the thought of "what would people say when she died?" By that evening, she decided to go about writing her own obituary. She'd write two, in fact. The first would be the obituary she wanted to have, and the second would be the one she would have if she kept doing what she was doing. This was an opportunity to lay bare her aspirations and perceived realities, to honestly look at two versions of herself and reflect on the life she really wanted.

Writing her first obituary was a breeze. In it, she described a woman who lived life fearlessly and dreamed big. She described a woman who lived life by her own measure and didn't "give a damn what anybody else thought." The act of writing this down allowed Roz to step out of herself and look at an idealized version that wasn't constrained by her current reality. It was a liberating experience. "My pen flew across the paper, and I could feel a new zest for life bubbling up inside me," she explains. "I felt energized and empowered, and excited about this life that could be mine, for even as I wrote, I started to believe that this fantasy could come true."

Then she started into her second obituary, describing the outcome of the life she was living. The energy that carried her so quickly through her first obituary had now drained away, only to leave a cold sense of apathy and indifference. She made it through a solid half page of writing and then gave up. "The second obituary described a conventional, ordinary life—pleasant, with a few moments of excitement," she says, "but leaving no legacy except a house sale and a few friends with fond memories."

It was a sobering realization for Roz. Everything she had been striving for in life wasn't making her happy, nor was it going to. "I realized then, that if I carried on living as I was, I would not end up with the life I wanted." So she set about making a change.

Over the coming months and years Roz Savage would change her life completely. "I admitted to myself that my story of success was the wrong one for me, and then I let go of all the manifestations of that. I moved out of the house. I left my husband. I left my management consulting job. I let go of all of those things that represented security."

Writing her potential obituary was the catalyst that started a new life for her, and it gave her fresh insight. She didn't know yet where she wanted to go, but now she knew exactly where she didn't. "For the previous 15 years I had been bound by obligations and duty," she says in her book *Rowing the Atlantic: Lessons Learned on the Open Ocean,*[1] "and for the first time in my life I felt free." She was now on a new path, a path to find her purpose. And she approached it with gusto.

"I call it my 'happy dabbling' phase," she explains, "I was a photographer. I was an organic baker. I was going to open a coffee shop. I was going to buy this tugboat and make it a live-aboard. I wrote a book. I tried on many different things and learned from those various experiences what brought me joy and what didn't." She had aspirations, too. "I wanted to see more of this planet before we degraded it even further. I wanted to find out who I was when I was alone—when I was not reacting to the expectations of others. Most important, I wanted to make a contribution to the greater good."

Roz got her first taste of real adventure in 2003 when she traveled to Peru on her own for an extended three-month exploring, trekking, and mountaineering trip. The journey boosted her confidence in her ability to survive, and even thrive, in an ever-changing environment, and it was here, in the thin air of the Peruvian Andes, that she had her first epiphany in finding her purpose. "I saw the extent of retreating glaciers in the mountains of Peru and it shocked me. The thought that this could happen so quickly was an eye-opener. I found my environmental mission right away—there it was. Climate change was no longer a concept to me, it was reality. I needed to convey this message."

You may find Roz's actions astonishing or even extreme. Changing everything in her life yet still having no sense of where she was going does seem extreme, but as we discussed in our chapter exploring grit, finding purpose manifests itself during the process of exploration, and not at the start of it. If curiosity is the budding seed in spring, then purpose is the bountiful crop harvested in fall. Roz was discovering her purpose her own way, and now after her Peru journey, she knew that an environmental message had to be part of it.

Her sense of purpose came to her driving along the highway in her camper van on a sunny English summer day in 2004. "I remember the precise moment," she says. "I wasn't thinking about anything in particular," and then suddenly, "Flash! I know! I'll row the Atlantic! I nearly veered off the highway when the thought hit me."

What she didn't realize at the time was this inspiration, this seemingly crazy idea of doing something completely beyond her discernible capacity, started her on the road to becoming an internationally recognized adventurer and arguably the world's greatest ocean rower of all time. She had found her way toward purpose.

According to developmental psychologist Bill Damon, "In data set after data set there's a pattern. Everyone has a spark. And that's the very beginning of purpose. That spark is something you're interested in."[2] Roz had found her spark of an idea—to row an ocean—and she was on the road to find her purpose.

Roz Savage rowing in the Moloka'i Channel, Hawaii   *Courtesy of Roz Savage*

Back to the Basics

How do you feel about the word *purpose*? Does it intimidate you, overwhelm you, or even scare you? For many people, *purpose* is a weighted word. Finding that "one big thing" to chase, that one thing that will give your life absolute fulfillment, is a daunting prospect for many of us.

Bringing it back to its basics, the concept of purpose is a cognitive process that helps define life goals and provides personal meaning. Devoting effort and making progress toward goals that are aligned to a purpose can give people a renewable, almost limitless source of intrinsic engagement and meaning.

Breaking down purpose into a process and talking about it in clear and discernible language is important. It makes finding purpose more accessible and tangible to us, rather than esoteric. After all, this book is intended to be pragmatic and applicable. Clarity in language and thinking will help to that end.

There's a wonderful parable about purpose that brings it to life.

A traveler comes upon three bricklayers at a building site and asks, "What are you doing?"

The first man says, "I am laying bricks."
The second man says, "I am building a church."
And the third man says, "I am building the house of God."

The first bricklayer has a job. The second has a career. The third has a calling—he has purpose.

Most of us readily associate with the first two bricklayers because in many ways, they are doing what we do. We perform a task that's our job, and we build an expertise at performing that task, turning it into a career. To that end, we are very similar to the bricklayers, but it's in the vision of the third bricklayer that something special happens and that most of us aspire to. For the third bricklayer, his career has transcended his act of doing and has become something much more. He has discovered a higher purpose to his actions.

Purpose, at its most basic, is about developing personal meaning. It's about contributing to something greater than yourself that exceeds your efforts.[3] Organizations that are purpose-driven are shown to have workers who exhibit superior levels of performance. These workers demonstrate more engagement and more ethical behavior; they are more readily adaptable to change and uncertainty and are more likely to align behind goals. Workers at purpose-driven organizations are better decision-makers, are more fulfilled in their work, and overall are higher performers than their counterparts in non-purpose-driven environments.

Connecting employees with purpose brings measurable business impact. Research from the EY Beacon Institute and Harvard Business School indicates that companies that lead with purpose are more likely to be profitable. Fifty-eight percent of companies with clearly understood purpose statements experienced growth of 10 percent plus.[4]

Corporate leaders generally have a strong vision and strategy on how they want to lead a business but typically don't possess a clear purpose to underpin that direction. One notable exception is Ajay Banga, the CEO of Mastercard, who has orchestrated the direction of this 12-billion-dollar company for the last 9 years and has developed a purpose-driven culture that espouses "do well by doing good." Banga's belief is that your interests and the interests of others don't have to be separated, that the individual and the organization can partner to be a force for good.

Banga's passion is to bring disadvantaged people into the financial mainstream, and he has led Mastercard with this core belief. His vision of a "world without cash" may seem like a self-serving attempt to corner the card and payments market, but for Banga the intent was to drive global financial inclusion. By removing cash and opening the digital payments space, he was able to give the poorest people access to the financial markets—both the capital and insurance markets—and allow them to participate. His actions reduced corruption and illicit trade as well because these criminal activities thrive in a cash-based market. Employees at Mastercard were inspired by Banga's passion around his purpose and his straightforward way of talking about it. He genuinely espoused his purpose, articulated it clearly, and was a great example of understanding a personal purpose and staying true to it. When behaviors are visibly demonstrated at the top of a company, people not only follow, they enthusiastically support and connect with a leader. Having a vision that's larger than yourself and larger than your company is what purpose-driven leadership looks like and is something that Ajay Banga has built for Mastercard.

At the company level, an authentic alignment to purpose is key. People can sense when a leader does not genuinely live his or her purpose, and when behaviors don't align with a purpose statement, it can backfire spectacularly. One of the best recent examples of this is Volkswagen Motors. In 2016, Volkswagen had made huge inroads into the environmentally conscious car market in the United States. The company had successfully promoted their diesel cars as a legitimate alternative to the electric and hybrid car market as a way to make an impact in environmental stewardship. With their incredibly low emissions, these vehicles brought a real environmentally friendly option at an attractive price point. VW used their reputation for quality to quash any doubt around the seemingly impossible performance metrics of the cars and quickly became a leader in the green vehicular marketplace. Unfortunately, it was indeed too good to be true.

Nearly half a million Volkswagen vehicles were found to have a so-called defeat device that tricked the software of the Environmental Protection Agency emissions testing to register lower readouts. The very vehicles that were being marketed as environmental game-changers were producing pollutants 40 times over the allowable limit in the United States.[5]

The CEO at the time, Martin Winterkorn, had been sent a memo nearly a year earlier pointing out the discrepancies, but nothing was done to remedy the situation. Winterkorn maintained his innocence, claiming the memo had never been read, and quickly blamed lower-level software engineers for installing the devices. Under Winterkorn's leadership, VW had set the stage for people with high intelligence and low ethics to drive profitability and growth. The company's goal was to sell cars at any cost and their environmental stand was simply a ruse. Volkswagen quickly lost all consumer confidence and has become a disheartening business example of a company with the opposite of a purpose-driven vision.

But Volkswagon's bad behavior has not become a trend, and in 2019, purpose-driven leaders and organizations are finding themselves at the forefront, demonstrating that success for a business can go beyond shareholder profits. Marc Benioff, CEO of Salesforce, is great example of a purpose-driven leader who has shaped the culture of his company. "Companies can do more than just make money," says Benioff. "They can serve others [too]."[6] Right from its inception in 1999 Benioff incorporated philanthropy into the day-to-day life at Salesforce and made it his mandate to ensure that the company serves all stakeholders, not just shareholders. From setting aside profit and product to help underserved communities to establishing requisite volunteer time among its employees, Benioff has defined Salesforce's purpose not to be just about improving the bottom line, but also about improving the state of the world.[7]

The trend now is toward purposeful impact versus shareholder profit as a benchmark of success for the largest global companies. This is evidenced by the ground-breaking Business Roundtable Statement of Purpose signed by 181 CEOs in August 2019. The statement recognizes that deeper purpose attracts customers, motivates talent, and resonates with shareholders. As Alex Gorsky, the CEO of Johnson & Johnson and the chair of the Roundtable, put it, "There is an essential role corporations can play in improving our society when CEOs are truly committed to meeting the needs of all stakeholders."

Having Purpose Is Good for You, Personally

Purpose is that feeling we have when we are working in alignment with our intrinsic motivational goals. The feeling is biologically generated by two neurochemicals, oxytocin and dopamine, which the brain releases to help reward behaviors that are valued for our survival.[8] Oxytocin is a connection hormone, and dopamine drives the reward network in our brain. The clarity of understanding why you do what you do has a long-reaching impact on your physiology and may, indeed, affect the quality and quantity of your life.[9]

What if finding purpose in your life could reduce your risk of dementia or stroke? The seemingly unlikely relationship has become less so over the last decade as researchers have begun to look at purpose through a biological lens to determine its impact on the brain. The focus of much of the research is in an area called purpose in life (PIL), introduced to the field of psychiatry in the 1940s by Austrian neurologist and psychiatrist Viktor Frankl.

Frankl, a Holocaust survivor, endured three agonizing years in Nazi concentration camps during WWII, including the living hell that was Auschwitz. In his best-selling book *Man's Search for Meaning*, he discusses the importance of finding meaning in all forms of existence, even the most horrific ones. His words are prophetic. "Man's main concern is not to gain pleasure or to avoid pain but rather to see a meaning in his life. That is why man is even ready to suffer, on the condition, to be sure, that his suffering has meaning."

Frankl's work has spawned modern clinical research around PIL that looks at the biological manifestations of purpose. Researcher Patricia Boyle at Rush Alzheimer's Disease Center is the principal researcher in a study indicating that having a greater PIL may, in fact, hinder the harmful effects associated with Alzheimer's disease. Her research suggests that those with a high PIL were only half as likely to develop Alzheimer's and were 30 percent less likely to develop mild cognitive impairment (a condition that sometimes progresses to Alzheimer's). That purpose contributes to avoidance of health issues later in life is really only one reason to think more deeply about your own purpose.

In her paper, "Oh What Happiness! Finding Joy and Purpose Through Work," scholar Joan Marques of Woodbury University in Burbank, California, states that finding a meaningful purpose is more enduring than happiness and can sustain people through periods of stress and suffering. Marques suggests that when we chase happiness instead of purpose and meaning, we often struggle, as demonstrated by the growing numbers of workforce members suffering from depression, chronic dissatisfaction, and a wide range of psychosomatic symptoms.[10] These symptoms also impact the discretionary effort people apply to their jobs. Without a purpose, motivation drops and people complete what they "have to do," instead of creating an environment where they "want to do," going above and beyond their work because they care. When the work becomes particularly hard, a lack of purpose often causes attrition—why stay at a job that provides neither purpose or happiness?

The desire for purposeful work is a fundamental human need, according to Aaron Hurst, the author of *The Purpose Economy*. Hurst, the founder of Taproot Foundation, an organization that creates volunteer opportunities for business people to impact nonprofits, suggests that the driver of our new economic era is connecting people to their purpose. Millennials are moving away from traditional career paths to find more meaning in what they do; a sharing economy has started to burgeon from cars, to bikes, to where we live. Hurst argues there's a new awakening in the current economic era that is moving toward the greater good.

According to LinkedIn's global *Purpose at Work* study in 2016, 64 percent of purpose-oriented employees find higher levels of fulfillment in their work, 50 percent are more likely to be in leadership positions, and 47 percent are more likely to be promoted.[11] And for those of us who are millennials or who work with millennials, the study identified that 71 percent of this group ranked finding meaningful work as one of the top three factors in determining career success, with 30 percent of those in the study ranking it as number one.

How Do You Find and Define Your Purpose?

We've looked at purpose as a cognitive process and at why it's important for us. Our earlier stories show how essential purpose is at an organizational level and why a clarity of purpose is critical to bringing out the best in its employees. As a leader, one of the fundamental jobs is to not just communicate a purpose, but to authentically live and uphold that purpose statement. We've discovered that having purpose in life will help alleviate stress and suffering, will lead to greater well-being, and can hinder the debilitating effects associated with Alzheimer's disease and likely others. A desire for purpose appears to be a basic human need, and an expression of this is becoming ever more present in the new workplace. Nick Craig and Scott A. Snook argue, in their article "From Purpose to Impact" in the *Harvard Business Review*, that "the process of articulating your purpose and finding courage to live it . . . is the single most important developmental task you can undertake as a leader."[12] With the importance of finding our purpose so clear, how do we go about finding it?

Unfortunately, it's not that easy. And the statistics bear this out. In Craig and Scott's article they describe how they have trained thousands of managers over the years at organizations from GE to the Girl Scouts, as well as an equal number of students and executives at the Harvard Business School. And in all their training they've "found fewer than 20 percent of leaders have a strong sense of their own individual purpose. Even fewer can distill their purpose into a concrete statement."[13] But as we've illustrated, finding your purpose will allow you to become the best leader, and the best person, you can be.

Roz Savage   Courtesy of Roz Savage. Photo credit Doug de Mark

Let's take a look at Roz's experience and figure out how we can find our own purpose. Roz discovered after her obituary exercise that she was living out a life that was expected of her rather than a life she wanted to lead. She found her purpose by looking for who she really was, her real identity, her essence. It was unique and personal to her and no one else. As Craig and Scott put it, "It's not what you do, it's how you do your job and why—the strengths and passions you bring to the table no matter where you're seated."

Being present and self-aware can give us a leg up on finding our purpose. It took Roz a long time to finally come to terms with this, but when she did, there was no turning back. Following Roz's lead from her journey to find and fulfill her purpose, you can set yourself on a path by looking at three fundamental items to find and define your purpose:

1. **Find your spark.** Like Roz, there's little doubt you've had a time in your life where you've felt a powerful spark of interest. What was it for you? What did you love to do before the responsibilities of life took precedence? The spark is where it all begins, from where the budding flames of passion start, from where they eventually build into a bonfire of purpose. There are several different ways to find the elusive spark.

   Like Roz, you can head down the road of self-exploration. You can try different things and have a "happy dabbling phase" as Roz did. She tried being a photographer and a baker, she wrote a book, she contemplated opening a coffee shop, and even thought about buying a live-aboard tug boat. She tried all this and more, but when the idea of rowing the Atlantic struck her, she knew right away she'd found her spark.

   Maybe you can write the obituary you hope that gets written about you as Roz did, or you can take a less gloomy tact and reflect back on those moments in your childhood when you were your happiest and most engaged. Some of the following questions might help.

What did you love to do growing up? Are you creative or artistic by nature? Perhaps your work and life are infused with creative approaches to solving problems. Are you spending enough time thinking about and tackling those problems that excite and challenge you? Carve out 10 percent of your week to give time and space to think about how to solve those problems more creatively. Did you have a wild imagination as a child, creating scenarios and imaginary friends? Start a book club or brainstorming team, and gather people from all parts of your organization with different approaches to spend time with individuals who think differently than you. Have you always been an entrepreneur or intrapreneur in your organization, always creating new opportunities? Start a side hustle or innovation group, or even take the bold step of going off on your own. Maybe you love helping others, or organizing sports and games, and this has led you to be an enabler? How can you mentor and give back to others on your team, in your company, or in volunteer work? Spending time reflecting on those things that make you feel energized and alive, those things that define you in an elemental way and bring you joy, can lead you to an aha moment around what you really loved then and still love today. Finding ways to fulfill those passions both at work and beyond can help you experiment with what drives you.

Sometimes finding your spark comes from analyzing the most challenging experiences in your life and how they've shaped you. By reflecting back on the "crucible" experiences you've had, those moments that have challenged you beyond what you thought you were capable of, you can discover what has shaped you into the person you are today. What meaning can derive from those challenges?

For Roz Savage, finding her spark was done through the chance alignment of disparate passions and interests in her life that all became rationalized by her Atlantic row. She had been drawn to the boating community for a long time because of their expression of comradeship and unconventional lifestyle, and she'd always associated boat travel with adventure. She wanted to embark on an adventure and travel the world, but wanted to do so in an environmentally friendly way. She had tried her hand at marathon running and racing and was drawn to the idea of an even bigger physical challenge. By quitting her job and leaving her marriage, she was empowered by an increasing sense of self-reliance and she wanted to test this even more. And most important to her after her journey to Peru, she had an environmental message she wanted to share. Roz wanted to leave her mark in some way and create a legacy, leaving the world a slightly better place than it was before she arrived. The idea to row across the Atlantic Ocean rolled all these seemingly unrelated desires into one bold concept. She'd found her spark. With patience and focus, you can too.

2. **Align your spark with your core values.** Once Roz was hit with that spark of the idea to row the Atlantic Ocean, there was no turning back. She invested her life savings into purchasing an ocean rowing boat and set in motion what would prove to be a new life's course.

The very idea of a well-heeled management consultant, fresh off 11 years of corporate work, undertaking one of the most challenging ocean voyages on the planet seems a bit unbelievable, but not for Roz. She set about preparing for her journey in earnest, regardless of the fact that she was hopelessly inexperienced.

On November 3, 2005, 26 crews would set out from La Gomera on the Canary Islands as part of the Atlantic Rowing Race. Over the course of the following 3,000 miles, six boats would capsize or sink and never make it to Antigua. Roz would not be one of them.

Even though hopelessly out of her element at the start, Roz would adapt to the environment and the challenge it presented and discover a hidden talent for overcoming adversity. Over the course of her journey she would face the wrath of raging ocean storms and do so completely alone in the empty vastness of the Atlantic Ocean. She would struggle with a malfunctioning water-maker right from the beginning and would break all four of her oars over the course of her journey. Her camping stove would stop working on day 20 and she would eat her dried-food meals cold and poorly rehydrated from that point forward. On day 79 of her 103-day odyssey, her satellite phone would call it quits and she'd be left completely cut off from the outside world for the remaining part of her trip. But in this raw and inhospitable environment, Roz would thrive. By the time she arrived in Antigua, three and a half months after starting, she would discover that her spark of interest had built into a passion.

Her original idea for the journey was to be 50 percent personal growth and 50 percent environmental mission. She had been hugely motivated to use her row as a platform to proclaim her message, taking a systems approach to designing a sustainable and fulfilling future for our world. As the daughter of Methodist preachers, it would seem she had naturally absorbed the idea that there's something out there bigger than herself and inherited a natural proclivity to speak to it as well. "I was full of bumptious enthusiasm, overflowing with the zeal of the convert, and eager to do all I could to save the world. I had become a woman with a mission—but why would anybody listen? I needed a platform, a pulpit from which I could proclaim my message."

But she says, "As it turned out, the circumstances were so extremely challenging that personal growth ended up taking up around 90 percent of my bandwidth. I was having to work so hard just to survive and not go insane. Although the environmental mission was a huge motivation to keep on going, I felt that I didn't really do justice to that mission on the Atlantic."[14]

After successfully rowing the Atlantic, Roz set about rowing another ocean to get things right. This time she would face down the Pacific Ocean, an incredible 8,000-mile journey across the world's largest ocean. She had found her spark and passion, and it had become her "pulpit," as she put it. She needed to speak louder about her environmental mission and would use a world-record setting journey across the Pacific to do it.

What Roz was doing was cultivating her purpose by aligning what she is doing with her core values. She was consciously crafting her "job" as a rower to add more personal meaning to it, to imbue it with a deeper sense of purpose. It's something we can all do in our work.

Dr. Amy Wrzesniewski, professor of Organizational Behavior at the Yale School of Management, with researchers Jane Dutton and Gelaye Debebe, have studied how you can change your current work to enhance its connections to your core values. As part of their research, they studied hospital maintenance workers to look at how they crafted their work to enhance their experience and to better align with their values and sense of purpose. They looked at two groups of hospital cleaning staff to understand the nature of the meaning of their work, what they experienced in it, what they enjoyed, and what was lacking. What they found in their study stunned them.

In the first group, they found that the cleaners talked about their work exactly as you would expect them to. They didn't talk about it as a satisfying pursuit or requiring great skill, but rather in terms of the benefits of the work and the tasks involved, concrete examples of mopping, cleaning, taking out trash, and making sure they were accomplishing the tasks they were assigned in their job role. The second group, in contrast, talked about their work in very different terms. They enjoyed the work and felt that it required a high degree of skill. When asked what they were doing on the job, they described cleaning patients' rooms each day and monitoring how those patients were feeling—whether they were sad or lonely. And if they were, they would double back on their shift to spend some extra time with them. One cleaner talked about stopping their custodial work and personally walking the elderly visitors of the patients through the maze of corridors of the hospital back to their cars, which was an offense they could be fired for, just to ease the minds of the patients knowing that their loved ones were being taken care of. And another cleaner, working on a floor with coma patients, described how she routinely moved paintings between rooms just to liven things up, knowing full well that the patients were unresponsive. The reason she did this, she explained, was that she thought that by creating this change she may spark their recovery in some way. When asked if that was part of her job description, she replied, replied, "That's not part of my job, but that's part of me."[15]

What Dr. Wrzesniewski and her team discovered was this second group of workers influenced the scope of their work to add personal meaning to it. They call this practice "job crafting," and they define it as "what employees do to redesign their own jobs in ways that foster engagement at work, job satisfaction, resilience, and thriving."[16] The employees cognitively crafted their work, altering how they perceived the tasks they were doing and and the inherent meaning in those tasks. Just as the cleaner did who said her empathetic actions were not part of her job but rather part of her, we're all able to better align our core values with our work. Discovering your purpose is all about finding your spark and then over time, crafting it and aligning it with your values. It is something we can all do and is something Roz did intentionally on her second world-record-setting ocean row across the Pacific Ocean.

3. **Contribute to the greater good.** As Angela Duckworth says in her book *Grit: The Power of Passion and Perseverance*, "At its core, the idea of purpose is the idea that what we do matters to people other than ourselves."[17] It's creating a connection to something much bigger than us that is developed over time. "A calling is not some fully formed thing that you find," says Dr. Amy Wrzesniewski. "It's much more dynamic. Whatever you do—whether

you're a janitor or a CEO—you can continually look at what you do and ask how it connects to other people, how it connects to the bigger picture, how it can be an expression of your deepest values."[18]

For Roz Savage her evolution of her sense of purpose coincided with her evolution as an environmentalist. In rowing the Pacific Ocean, she was a woman on a mission proclaiming her environmental message from the "pulpit" that was the deck of her boat. In 2011, Roz rowed the Indian Ocean, becoming the first woman to solo row the "Big Three," the Atlantic, Pacific, and Indian Oceans. The crossing took her 154 days.

As Roz continued to row and continued to break records, she recognized her capacity to create positive change increased as well. Her lists of recognitions and awards are as long as they are impressive. She holds four Guinness World Records for ocean rowing. She is a member of the Order of the British Empire for services to environmental awareness and fundraising. She is a United Nations Climate Hero, a Fellow of the Royal Geographical Society, and a Fellow of the Explorers Club of New York. She is listed among the Top Twenty Great British Adventurers by the *Daily Telegraph* and the Top Ten Ultimate Adventurers by *National Geographic*. In 2010, she was named Adventurer of the Year by *National Geographic* and in 2011 received the Ocean Inspiration Through Adventure award. With all this recognition came a profound realization that she could use her significant fame to help others.

"Over the years of environmental messaging and thinking and campaigning, I've had a fundamental shift in thought. I love that Buckminster Fuller quote: *'You never change things by fighting against the existing reality. To change something, build a new model that makes the old model obsolete.'* Focus on positive solution rather than on the problem."[19]

In 2018, using her notoriety as a world-renowned explorer, Roz created her Sisters project as a way to give back to society by unifying the global community of women to create a better future. "The Sisters is my attempt of creating a new model that renders the existing model obsolete," she says emphatically. "I think that for a lot of women their inner critic is a lot stronger than it is for men, and there are too many women who feel that they don't have anything to add to these really vital conversations we need to be having right now. I'm hoping through the Sisters to activate more women to have the confidence and courage to contribute to the conversation. We need all hands on deck."[20]

Roz Savage has found her purpose and her rowing career was simply a means of getting her there. Roz's sense of purpose matured through her rowing career, with one idea being supported by the next, until she confidently felt that she personally can make a difference through her Sisters project. She feels now she can truly be in the service of others. Leadership consultant Morgan couldn't agree more.

Morgan spends much of her time working with others to help solidify their purpose, simplifying it in all aspects of their lives. She believes that operating with purpose at work and at home drives additional discretionary effort and allows us to go above and beyond in our day-to-day existence. We discussed her approach on purpose and noticed something very interesting.

"When people aren't working and living their purpose, they're often working from a standpoint of ego or scarcity," she says. "Either they are thinking about how something makes them look or feel, or operating from a place of concern and worry that they won't have something or will lose out." Morgan uses the prompt of asking people, when they are at their best at work, what have they been "in service of"? What she finds is that, the phrase "in service of" allows people to articulate why they show up. So like the bricklayer who goes from a job, to a career, to a calling "in the service of" God, think about what you are "in service of" when you're at your best and how might you be able to contribute to the well-being of others.

As Viktor Frankl said, "Being human always points, and is directed, to something or someone—other than oneself—be it a meaning to fulfill or another human being to encounter. The more one forgets himself—by giving himself to a cause or to another person to love—the more human he is."

CHAPTER 5

Innovation

Big Dreams and Big Struggles

ex Pemberton holds tightly to the grab bar above the helicopter cabin door. His feet are firmly planted on the skid below as the rotor blade screams just inches above his head. Beneath him, 10,000 feet of air to the sandy scrub of the Baja desert beckons below. The carbon-fiber wing attached to Rex's back transforms him into a human rocket, and for all intents and purposes, he is. "I had to pinch myself a thousand times before I jumped out of the helicopter," says Pemberton. "I asked myself, 'What the hell are you about to do?' It was ridiculous. It's like you're flying your own body."

Rex is feeling good and he's ready to go. His gut is telling him everything is OK. But he doesn't always feel this way. A year ago, just as he was about to leap from his helicopter on another parachuting feat, he felt something was very wrong. "I was on the side of the helicopter, and I just had this feeling like something was going to go wrong," he explains. "I'm not sure what it was. I had no idea what it could have been. I just had this wicked feeling that something was going to go wrong." His mission was to jump from the helicopter with a surfboard by his side and transition to surfing when he hit the water. "No one had ever transitioned from parachuting to surfing before!" he exclaims enthusiastically, his energy contagious. But apart from the obvious complexities of the jump, he felt something else was wrong. Rex ignored his gut feeling and jumped anyway. He freefell with his board at his side, opened his canopy, attached his surfboard to his feet, lined up a wave, and descended upon it. Once he touched the water, he released his chute and began to surf, making wide, arcing turns across the waves. He would proceed to jump five more times to perfect the stunt and capture it on film. The first five jumps had gone very well, and on the next try, Rex spotted the perfect wave. As he was readying to jump, the boat filming his stunt flipped in heavy surf and the photographers and driver were left fighting for their lives. "There was a whole huge rescue operation going on below me," he says. "I had no idea, but my gut told me something was wrong. I should have listened." Fortunately, no one was seriously injured among the film team, but the whole ordeal gave Rex a greater appreciation for his intuition.

But at this moment, high above the Baja desert, Rex's gut instinct is giving him the green light. He pushes away from the helicopter and drops into the yawning void of space below him. The feeling of freefall is overwhelming and induces a primal sensation of wanting to grab hold of anything to make it stop, but for Rex, this is a feeling he's accustomed to. He has skydived over 4,000 times, with 3,000 of those being wingsuit flights, so he naturally resists the sensation to flail and settles into the task at hand. However, this jump is different than his others. Attached to Rex's back is a six-foot-wide carbon-fiber wing with two small jet turbine engines affixed to it. The jetwing, as he calls it, weighs over 50 pounds and is hard to maneuver, but he soon steadies the wing and flicks on the jets. "It's a dream people have as kids to simply fly along in the clouds," he had said before his jump. Now for four minutes, Rex realizes that dream.

The evolution of Rex Pemberton from an adventure-hungry high school student to a groundbreaking extreme athlete is a fascinating one. It all started on a student leadership expedition to Peru when he and his classmates were given the opportunity to sign up for an expedition of their choice. "A group of us had to pick between climbing a mountain or going whitewater rafting, and we chose mountain climbing," he says. "We just saw this peak and we decided to climb it." The peak was the 19,000-foot Hualca Hualca and the students set about getting up it. Amazingly, two weeks later, they summited. "I'll never forget it. I remember standing on the top of this peak in Peru looking out over the

Amazon basin, and the sun was setting, and it was this beautiful moment when I thought, 'I love this climbing stuff,' and I wanted to climb the highest mountain in the world, Mount Everest."

Rex Pemberton dropping from a plane into a flight on his carbon-fiber jetwing

Courtesy of Rex Pemberton

Immediately upon returning home to Sydney, Australia, the young Pemberton set about pursuing his newfound dream of climbing Mount Everest with the zeal and naiveté that only a 16-year-old boy can muster. "I spent seven months secretly sending out sponsorship proposals, realizing the cost of the climb and what it would take before I even shared the idea with my mom and dad," he says. "I remember when I told my parents, I walked into the living room literally shaking with fear. My mom and dad were watching TV and I was afraid of what they might say. That at 16, I shouldn't do it, that I'm too young, that I'm not good enough, that I don't have enough experience, that

I should focus on school and university like everyone else. But I was really surprised by their reaction. They just kind of rolled with it and said, 'That's nice dear' and kept watching TV. They didn't take me seriously but a short time later, when I showed them my sponsorship proposals I sent out, they realized how damn serious I was."

Instead of trying to dissuade the eager teenager, the senior Pembertons set about helping their son. "My dad was a businessman and explained I needed to use better grammar in the proposal and that I needed to put in a return on investment strategy on it," he says. "My parents weren't going to hinder my dream, but instead they were going to help me. With the support of my family I was then able to get a platform of support from people around me who wanted to help me, and from that came the contacts to various different organizations and sponsorship."

It would take him several years of focus and effort, but by the age of 21, Rex summited Mount Everest, becoming the youngest Australian ever to do so. By age 23, he had become the third youngest person to complete the Seven Summits, reaching the highest point on every continent. But that was just the start for Rex in innovating in the adventure world.

Dream Big

Being innovative in business can be a terrifying process that often requires stepping into the unknown. Rex has been innovative in his own adventure career, moving from mountaineering into the unknown of flying his jetwing. And, much like Rex

Pemberton hanging off that helicopter over the Baja desert, individuals tasked at being innovative stare into a yawning void of uncertainty that wants to swallow them whole. Most of us have experienced it in one manner or another: we're asked to huddle up with our team, to brainstorm new ideas, and to come back with an innovative solution. Hackathons, ideation contests, and brainstorms have become the norm, particularly in technology companies who are considered at the forefront of innovation, and the pressure to perform can be intense. Quarterly cycles, short deadlines, and new competitive landscapes with startups taking over markets force the need for a continuous drive to innovate. But are those stress-filled petri dishes of experimentation really the best ways to drive innovation and new ideas?

Yes and no.

Innovation is a complicated process, and years of research show there are many methods of getting it right. It is related to, but not the same as, invention, and entails much the same process. Invention pertains to something that has never been made before, while innovation "is more apt to involve the practical implementation of an invention to make a meaningful impact in the market or society."[1] "One might say that the first telephone was an invention, the first cellular telephone either an invention or an innovation, and the first smartphone an innovation."[2] Both demand creativity, ideation, and insight, but as business professionals we are faced with needing to be innovative far more than needing to be inventive.

But how do we stimulate innovative thinking? All too often when a good idea happens or an innovation is created, it's attributed to individual genius, timing, or luck. The fixed mindset of associating innovative thinking to something elusive and out of our control is all too common and inhibiting. We are all capable of being innovative; the first step is dreaming big.

For Rex Pemberton, dreaming big has always been a key part of his adventure success. By his own account he has always allowed himself to fantasize more than other people. "If I have an interesting idea, I'll follow it and give myself the time and space to emotionally connect to it and explore it." What his daydreaming has allowed him to do is explore the possibilities and potential of an idea without shutting it down, stoking the curiosity, asking questions to dig deeper into the impossible, and increasing the processing time he needs to come up with an aha moment.

Intuitively, it makes sense that if you are stuck on a problem, allowing your mind to wander can help you come up with a solution. Think about when you come up with your best ideas; it's typically not sitting at your desk pouring over the problem, but on a walk, or driving to work, or even when you are in the shower. Those are spots where you often let your mind wander. In a 2009 a study published in the journal *Proceedings of the National Academy of Sciences* (PNAS) backs this intuition and suggests that areas of the brain used for complex thinking are stimulated when you are daydreaming. "Mind-wandering is typically associated with negative things like laziness or inattentiveness," says Kalina Christoff, a psychologist at the University of British Columbia. "But this study shows our brains are very active when we daydream—much more active than when we focus on routine tasks." The study indicates that daydreaming allows us to drift away from specific tasks at hand and allows us to better focus on the more complex problems that need solving.[3]

Taking that time and space as an individual or team to marinate on ideas is necessary for true aha moments. Like Rex, spending time in a truly creative space and allowing time to daydream allows your subconscious brain to combine and process novel thoughts. By daydreaming, your mind has an opportunity to connect ideas that may never have been connected in that way before, in a mental mash-up of sorts. "Many times the 'dialogue' that occurs, when the daydreaming mind cycles through different parts of the brain, accesses information that was dormant or out of reach," explains Eugenio M. Rothe, a psychiatrist at Florida International University. "This accounts for creativity, insights of wisdom and oftentimes the solutions to problems that the person had not considered."[4]

To daydream requires taking precious time from what is likely a hectic and busy, overscheduled day. It may feel like you are wasting your time when you are daydreaming, but the science says otherwise. Even though an aha moment feels quite instantaneous, it is actually the result of a fairly lengthy process of neurological connections over time. Generating true insight is primarily a subconscious process of connections being discovered and made. We need to disconnect one way of thinking to reconnect another way, and this takes time. Although in some cases, a hackathon yields amazing results for a company, more often than not, it is a result of a person or team having spent time and space considering the idea well before the challenge. The brainstorming session serves mostly as a way to unearth those great big ideas or take those fledgling ideas to the next level.

An important component of innovation closely associated to daydreaming is the idea of incubation time. Insights seen as truly creative often result from a process whereby initial conscious thought is followed by a period during which one refrains from thinking about that specific challenge consciously. This period of incubation essentially allows the unconscious processes in the brain to contribute to creative thinking and insight or aha formation. Incubation does not necessarily mean thinking idly, but rather taking and working on something completely different to enhance the incubation affect versus doing something similar to the insight-related task.[5] The unconscious processes of daydreaming and incubation help in stimulating creative and divergent thinking and are core to the insight process.[6]

There are a number of companies dedicated to pushing the envelope of innovation, and Google is one of the leaders. As a company, Google has made a concentrated effort to resurrect the lost art of innovation and invention, and in so doing has created a secret laboratory they call X. Like something right out of a James Bond movie, Google X is a so-called moonshot factory and is trying "to demystify and routinize the entire process of making a technological breakthrough—to nurture each moonshot, from question to idea to discovery to product—and, in so doing, to write an operator's manual for radical creativity."[7] In setting their vision, Google X's hope is to incubate ideas beyond incremental thinking and to "create radical new technologies to solve some of the world's hardest problems."[8] Google X is there to dream big and to focus on innovation and invention. They drive toward 10x solutions, not 10 percent solutions, and are the prime example in dreaming big come to life. Some Google X projects include Internet balloons, energy kites, salt-based energy storage, and seawater fuel, to name a few. According to Bernard Meyerson, IBM's chief innovation officer, "A successful grand challenge is one that people, even experts in the field, regard as an epiphany and (*one that*) challenges assumptions about what's possible."[9] It would appear Google X is doing exactly this.

When was the last time you spent time challenging the assumptions of what is possible in your role, your team, or your organization? Very often, making large-scale changes is seen as an unwelcome challenge, but reworking your habitual approach to the larger problems that your team or company is trying to solve can be a way for you to take a Google X approach to your work. If a change happens in your business, say, a new technology has been introduced that digitally transforms your industry, or a new competitor enters the scene with a more nimble and agile approach to customers, or even a revamp of your internal operations, by pausing and recognizing that the change is an opportunity to improve and innovate, you'll put yourself in the right frame of mind for insightful thinking. It's often difficult to look at a challenge this way, but it's essential we do.

When we have processes that work for us and are deeply ingrained habits, it is often difficult for us to change those habits to innovate. Making a change to be more innovative is difficult, especially when things are working well. We often perceive change as negative, because as humans, our biology is tuned to look out for anything dangerous and out of the ordinary. This innate tendency has protected us and is a primary reason we have become the successful species we are today. But recognizing our negative tendencies is very important, because that little (or not so little) pessimistic voice in our heads can hinder our innovative thinking. In business, we all too often act on this instinct and focus on what might go wrong rather than what might be. Having the wherewithal to recognize this in your thoughts and actions is a first step in finding your own personal moonshot factory. Think about the last time your team, function, or organization made a change to a habit or process it had been using for a long period of time. Maybe a new, more efficient expense system was introduced, or the documentation for how to capture customer interactions changed. Perhaps it was as simple as changing the day or the time of a regular meeting you attend. What was your initial reaction? Was it annoyance at the inconvenience that the change presented? Maybe it was confusion as to why the change was made in the first place or irritation that you will be required to learn and do something new. Even those small negative tendencies when presented with a change can trip us up.

As you grow in your role and develop expertise, your capabilities build, as do your habits on how you get your work done. Maybe you become the established expert, so following your habits has paid off—even other people want to work as you do. Sometimes that is how a company establishes dominance in a market, doing the same thing extremely well. But what happens when a new entrant comes in with a new way of working? Often, the established company relies on their own tried-and-true experience and this can backfire. From Nokia to Kodak, Blockbuster to Yahoo, there are many examples of organizations who collectively didn't move from their comfort zone to think about continuous innovation. On an individual level, the best leaders continue to challenge themselves and how they work, even in those well-established habit and expertise areas.

As Rex Pemberton grew older, he began to evolve. He'd spent formative years climbing up mountains and doing everything he could not to fall off them, but something changed. He still wanted to climb up them, but now instead of climbing back down, he wanted to fly off them instead.

One of the most inspiring things about Rex's character is his natural enthusiasm and his childlike curiosity. "I've always had a strong sense of curiosity," he explains. "I think so many people shut down their sense of curiosity up front, thinking 'my ideas aren't good enough,' or 'I'm too young,' or 'I'm not experienced enough.' It's curiosity that gets you there. It gives you the license to experiment." When Rex discovered the perilous sports of BASE jumping and wingsuit flying, his curiosity was piqued and there was no turning back. Rex began to train as a parachutist and soon was leaping from cliffs, donning a specially constructed fabric wingsuit that allowed him to glide for several miles before deploying his parachute and landing. It was an exciting evolution for him, taking to the air, but one that he felt was perfectly natural. "You're always taught as a mountaineer and as a rock climber to hang on, to not fall off, because falling off is failure and could mean death. But once I learned how to fall, I became less scared of it. I got good at the falling. It became natural and part of the process; it helped my climbing massively." Failing and falling is a mandatory part of true innovation. Getting comfortable with failure, dusting yourself off, learning how to improve, and trying again is the key to innovating on an individual level. Accepting failure and recognizing that the lessons learned from it can actually inform our innovation process is a difficult pivot to accept and challenges many of us.

Rex Pemberton in the Himalayas on his record-setting Mount Everest summit bid

Courtesy of Rex Pemberton

And Rex, perpetually the dreamer, would continue to evolve. After becoming one of the most experienced wingsuit pilots on the planet, he transformed again. This time Rex, with a group of engineers and friends, began developing a futuristic jetpack that tossed the traditional concept of human-powered flight on its head. "I was deeply interested in expanding the envelope of human flight and thinking outside the box," he says. "I wanted to see it evolve." And so began his X-wing project. It began as the X-1, a simple plywood outline of Rex that was strapped to a wooden cutout of a wing that, over the next eight years of trial and error, developed into a carbon-fiber delta wing with high-tech electronics and miniature jet engines that is called the X-13. "This is something in my life I won't put on a shelf," explains Rex when asked about the project. "I think we will evolve this and the technology for a long time to come. I think the future of powered individualized human flight is going to be limitless."

The Struggle Is Real

Over the course of the last eight years, as he has transitioned to his current passion of jet-propelled flight, Rex, like many innovators, has confronted a myriad of challenges. In his climbing days, he had to face people in his life, including his parents and family, who questioned relentlessly, "Why risk your life to climb a mountain?" and it caused him a lot of pain. He had to face the reality that the choices he was making were affecting others, and he had to reflect on why he was doing what he was doing and if it was worth the risk. But now with his new pursuits, the challenges have evolved as well. "These days, I'm facing more tactical issues and struggles related to the jet wing," he says. "It's not so much a matter of why—at this point, my family and friends know this is part of who I am. Now, it's thinking more about the struggles in execution. Currently, you could objectively call parts of my project a failure. There have been times when the team and I have questioned ourselves and asked why? Why are we doing this? Why are we passionate about evolving flight? And I've started to reframe what failure really means to me. If you give up on something, to me, that's a failure, but making mistakes and learning from them, which is where I am at right now with the jet wing project, that isn't failure, that's learning from your mistakes."

It turns out, true innovation requires struggle.

"Failure sucks, but instructs."[10] This is the motto used by Bob Sutton and Diego Rodriguez, instructors and cofounders of Stanford University's d.school, one of the top innovative design schools in the world. Making mistakes and learning from them is a critical part of the innovation process. The failure paradox is that we often have more failures when we have more successes, and insight is more likely to emerge as more failures are experienced. Failure is seen as an F word by most businesses. It's seen as a liability, as a time suck, as a money waster, and as a reputation wrecker. But failure needs to be recognized for what it really is: as a natural byproduct and learning outcome of the creative process. In their article "Promoting Insightful Problem Solving," Pamela Ansburg and Roger Dominowski suggest that insightful problem solving is, in fact, facilitated by failure.[11] The more we try to avoid failing, the more we drift away from original thinking. The reality is that failure feeds insight, and it must be embraced for innovative thought.

Currently, most organizations spend less than 5 percent of their time on activities that generate new ideas.[12] This stigma associated with failing is often too much for them. With failure comes risk and with risk comes stress. This is something organizations typically try to avoid, but in avoiding failure, companies are losing their innovative edge. The mindset needs to shift.

Stress and struggle are part of the creative process and need to be embraced to be at our innovative best. Being more tolerant of risk and failure should become an organizational goal.

The optimal environment for innovative thinking, according to Dr. Lutfihak Alpkan of the Istanbul Technical University in his article "Organizational Support for Intrapreneurship and Its Interaction with Human Capital to Enhance Innovative Performance," is to empower so-called intrapreneurs within a corporate culture to take risk and to innovate. "We can suggest that top managers prioritizing on innovativeness should invest to build such an organizational milieu where first of all, support and tolerance exist to a large extent. Every employee should feel and know that if they behave like intrapreneurs and develop viable but still risky ideas for innovation and entrepreneurship, they will be supported in their firms, their proposals will be listened to, they will be encouraged for implementing their ideas with necessary emotional, physical, and monetary assistance, and even if their ideas and projects fail, they will not be punished or humiliated. Fears of loneliness and failure seem to be important burdens on the way to start and implement innovative projects, even if some clever ideas come to mind. An internal environment promising support and tolerance will be a good remedy for these fears."[13]

Sure, it sounds easy to unleash people and teams on creative projects and tell them failure is part of the process. But what does that look like in actual innovative companies? In an effort to find examples of real-world innovation, we spoke with Frankie Callahan, a senior program manager at AppDynamics. Prior to working at AppDynamics, Frankie spent eight years at Google and five years at Facebook, watching the latter grow from 1,100 employees to over 20,000. It's clear she is very familiar with innovative companies transforming into innovation powerhouses. Her job focuses on how people develop the ability to be creative, and she says, "empowering people who are passionate about solving a problem, and giving them autonomy, space, and time is key. [As a company] it's about being fearless, not reckless. Lifting away that fear of failure. Part of it is the accountability around innovation—that it's not unbound freedom, but the expectation that innovation will add value and change the way something is working. At the core of it, understanding that failure is OK and part of the process. We learn from it as long as we are working in service of the bigger picture." As part of that process, AppDynamics has its own innovation lab, allowing for experimental partnerships both internally and externally to allow innovation to flourish.

The Environment to Innovate

At his most creative, Rex says he is, "away from the stress of the day-to-day. I travel so often for work and spend hours and hours in meeting and conference rooms. When I'm not working, I like to plug into an environment that I love. Whether that's on a mountain or rock face or sailing, I'm definitely in nature. Sometimes it's on a long hike to a BASE-jumping spot. I always come up with my best ideas when I'm outside."

As Rex innately recognizes, your physical surroundings have a huge impact on your ability to foster creativity and innovation, and Dr. David Rock, the director of the NeuroLeadership Institute, has done research to prove this. Collaborating with a large health care firm, Rock, and his team of researchers conducted a study of 6,000 people, asking them where, when, and how they did their best thinking. Interestingly, only 10 percent of respondents said it happened at work.[14] It would appear that most of us come up with our best ideas not sitting at our desks but rather when we distance ourselves from the problem in some way. But likely this is not surprising for many of us. Maybe taking a page from Rex's book about getting into nature could be the key to setting ourselves up for more innovative thinking?

Rex Pemberton flies his carbon-fiber jetwing across the desert landscape on a test flight

Courtesy of Rex Pemberton

Nature provides an expansive environment for thought and induces a creative state more readily than a confined space. The colors of nature, primarily blue and green, tend to promote insight generation as well. The concept of "blue-sky thinking" is actually more grounded in reality than you might imagine as both the colors of the outdoors and its wide-open spaces foster open-minded thought.

But creative thinking is not limited only to nature and being aware of your built surroundings will help nurture those creative juices as well. High ceilings, natural light, and views to the outside all subconsciously broaden thought patterns to include remote associations.[15] Those associations can foster the combinations of ideas needed for true aha moments. One cannot overestimate the importance of our environment, natural or built, for the promotion of intuition and creativity.

In the 1950s, polio was an epidemic in the United States and became one of the most feared diseases countrywide. "In 1952 alone, nearly 60,000 children were infected with the virus; thousands were paralyzed, and more than 3,000 died."[16] Polio was the most serious communicable disease among US children and had become a national tragedy. During this time, in a small laboratory in the University of Pittsburg, a young researcher named Jonas Salk was working tirelessly to find a cure. He worked like a man possessed. The world needed a vaccine, and he knew he might have the answer. He was very close to finding a cure but couldn't quite put it all together. No matter how hard he worked or how hard he tried, he would always face the same roadblock. With a mix of frustration and angst, Salk took a vacation and traveled to the hill country of central Italy looking for an environment as far removed from Pittsburgh as he could find. He would frequent a thirteenth-century Franciscan basilica during his stay, as a place of introspection and respite. The Basilica di San Francesco d'Assisi is a spectacular building with whitewashed brick walls, magnificent frescoed ceilings, and soaring, light-drenched spaces. It was there, in this environment, that Jonas Salk realized he had the answer to his riddle. He immediately returned to his lab in Pittsburgh, revamped his experiments, and discovered the vaccine for polio.

Salk firmly believed that the environment he was in, the architecture of the basilica, inspired his discovery. Eight years later he would go on to create the world-famous Salk Institute of Biological Studies in La Jolla, California, choosing Louis Kahn, one of the most brilliant architects of the twentieth century, to help realize his vision. Salk had learned from personal experience that by skillfully crafting the built environment you work in, you can influence the insight and inspiration you garner there. The Salk Institute, one of the most celebrated pieces of modern architecture ever built, is a shining example of this.

As an award-winning architect himself, our coauthor Kevin Vallely deeply understands the power of architecture to transform the way we feel, think, and act. "This is my wheelhouse," he says. "Crafting our built environment is something we can all do readily ourselves. We just have to know what to do." Basilicas and research institutes are wonderful illustrations of grand architectural gestures that allow us to transcend our regular way of thinking, but as much as these macro acts have the power to affect our thinking, so too do more micro actions as well. "Employing dim lighting in a room to obscure physical details will increase abstract thinking and enhance bigger picture idea generation," says Vallely. Introducing elements in a space that promote softness, calmness, and openness will reduce threat states in our psyche and prime our brain for more remote associations.[17] Working in quiet, acoustically insulated spaces has an impact on our thinking and contributes to an insight-generating environment.[18] "Even just changing your location will help stimulate the insight generation process," says Vallely. "Move to another room, head outside, or down to the café. Whatever. If you're stuck, just move. It'll help." The idea is to trigger new associations in the brain, in any way we can, to stimulate innovative thinking. So with all this in mind, maybe your next brainstorming session should be on a plush-cushioned couch, looking out the window, in the lobby of your office building.

Now as much as our physical atmosphere is important for our innovative thinking, so too is our organizational atmosphere. A positive organizational atmosphere provides employees with a sense of commitment and motivation that facilitates innovativeness and creativity and can be boosted by the emotional intelligence (EI) of the people working there. In their article "Emotional Intelligence and Employee Creativity: Moderating Role of Proactive Personality and Organizational Climate," University of Bhutan researchers suggested people who are aware of their emotions and the emotions of others "promote more flexible, divergent thinking and related cognitive processes that facilitate the generation of novel and useful ideas."[19] Their research indicates that the effective use of emotions facilitates reasoning, decision making, and most important, problem solving, something at the heart of true innovation.

People with high emotional intelligence tend to be more open to unfamiliar situations and willing to take risks for new experiences and perspectives. Having employees with a high EI will help boost creative thinking in the workplace. If an organization deems creativity and innovation to be important to their culture, then their leaders must prioritize these elements as skills for their teams to master through experience, training, close monitoring, and support. Leaders who prioritize and care about innovation happening on their watch are critical for developing an organizational climate that will foster better innovation.[20]

Rex Pemberton is an upbeat guy, almost always with a big smile on his face. His easygoing nature is the first thing you notice when you meet him. He's always looking on the bright side of things and is always planning the next biggest and best adventure, no matter what it might be. We asked him what special something allows him to be this way, and he was very succinct in his answer. "Bottom line—life is such an amazing gift," he says. "I don't want to be too cliché, but life is really an amazing gift. And if you've got a goal, why not just go after it? I want to experience as much as I possibly can in life, right now, and that means following my passions, whether it's rock climbing, mountaineering, wing suiting, jet winging, corporate training, whatever it is. Just giving it a shot. I don't need to be the subject matter expert in anything or the very best; I just want to do a multitude of things, to have as much experience across a broad range of cool activities as I can. That's what I live for!"

Psychologists at Northwestern University in Illinois suggest, through their research, that a positive mood has one of the strongest impacts in generating more and better insights. In their article "A Brain Mechanism for Facilitation of Insight by Positive Affect," they write, "Participants higher in positive mood solved more problems, and specifically more with insight, compared with participants lower in positive mood."[21] A positive mood increases big picture focus and allows more cognitive flexibility, increasing the chance of suddenly switching attention and being open to a wider variety of potential solutions, while a negative mood, including anxiety and depression, narrows your scope of attention and is associated with deficits in cognitive control mechanisms.[22] Simply put, people solve insight and creative problems better when in a positive mood.

Realistically, most of us find it difficult to maintain a positive mood when we are struggling to find the answer to a challenge or under pressure to innovate. How does this kind of stress impact innovation? It is more complicated than just a positive–negative duality that exists, and one piece of research opens up space for the usefulness of criticality in innovation. In the article by George and Zhou, "Understanding When Bad Moods Foster Creativity and Good Ones Don't: The Role of Context and Clarity of Feelings," the authors write, "Sometimes people in negative moods may push themselves to come up with creative ideas because that negative mood can cause a deeper level of critical thinking and discernment."[23] Recognizing and awareness of your mood before taking on a creative project is an important takeaway. During the daydreaming state, a more positive take on your challenge is helpful. While working through a solution, however, you can relax if you have a more negative mood, as it will allow you to dig deeper and separate the good ideas from the bad.

In our conversation with senior program manager Frankie Callahan of AppDynamics, she made it clear to us how important it was to maintain an innovative environment in her company. "We were recently acquired by Cisco," she says, "but we still wanted to maintain the 'startup' environment we were used to having before the acquisition." In the last five years, the trend in Silicon Valley has been for larger, more established companies to acquire a startup and then allow the startup to operate relatively independently after acquisition. Integrating fresh ideas, new talent, more agile decision making and processes, and innovation culture while taking advantage of the established company's lessons learned, customers, and scale can work incredibly well for both companies (barring any culture clashes). AppDynamics took it one step further, using new resources to create an "Innovation Lab" to partner both internally as well as experiment externally with customers. Creating the environment for innovation and tolerance for failure can propel new ideas.

How can you set yourself and your organization up to generate more innovative ideas?

1. **Dream BIG.** Flying in formation with a helicopter at 4,500 feet over the Baja desert, under complete control, Rex Pemberton realizes his own dream of human flight

has become a reality. "In less than 10 years' time, I think you'll strap on a wing with built-in telemetry and thrust vectoring and we will literally be able to take off outside our houses and fly to a friend's 20 miles away," he says. "We'll be able to land vertically in their garden, just like Iron Man." You need to be a dreamer to innovate!

2. **Embrace the struggle.** Like Rex, you, too, will face your share of challenges and naysayers as you try to be more innovative. Recognizing and anticipating that struggle is part of the innovation process and helps buffer the effects when it hits. Struggle is a necessary part of the innovation game.

3. **Adjust your environment.** It turns out we have control over a diverse series of environmental triggers that can help foster new ideas. From the physical attributes of the spaces we work in to simply getting outside, or from our personal mood to the culture of our organization, the environment we work in and how we adjust to it will directly influence our insight and creativity.

CHAPTER 6

Resilience

Bouncing Forward

It was April 3, 2017, and Lisa Blair was awoken by a deafeningly loud bang from outside her cabin. She was sailing her racing yacht *Climate Action Now* through a storm on the Southern Ocean and had finally lain down for some rest.

"I bolted out of bed and looked out my dome," she recalls, referencing the acrylic dome that protrudes through the roof of her yacht's cabin. "I had this clear view outside. My mast, which is 22 meters long (66 feet), was just shaking from side to side like a snake in the air because there was no support in the middle of the mast. I knew at that point I had broken a piece of rigging wire and I needed to change direction, like, yesterday. This was serious."

For Lisa, it had been a storm like many others on her journey, with large messy seas and 40-knot winds relentlessly hammering her boat. These conditions were exhausting her mentally and physically, and they were due to get worse. She had noticed that the barometer was still falling, and by her estimate, the storm hadn't reached its climax yet. Her boat seemed to be handling the conditions well, and she needed to grab a nap before nightfall. This was her cue to get some rest.

Throughout the past 72 days, everything had been going exactly to plan for Lisa and she was now on track to break the world record for the fastest solo, nonstop sailing circumnavigation of Antarctica. She was one month away from reaching her goal and, after eating a hot meal and lying down, she stole a moment to think about what it would be like to finish her wild adventure and return home. She was lost in positive thought as she drifted off to sleep. That sudden, loud bang would change everything.

Lisa fumbled for her life jacket and made for the cabin door only to hear the mast snapping outside. "It's a sound I'll never forget," she recalls. "It's not like one bang and it's over, but it's this long drawn-out process of 30 seconds of screeching and groaning and everything is shuddering, the whole boat was flexing and twisting. I stood there with my eyes closed as I listened, my whole body was tense as my afternoon went from a pleasant sleep to scrambling for survival."

In a state of panic, Lisa emerged from the cabin and entered a world of complete mayhem. "The mast snapped at deck level, so there was nothing standing up outside my boat, it was totally gone," she recalls. The mast had fallen to the leeward side of the boat, pushed over by the wind, and immediately became an immovable object in the water. *Climate Action Now* instantly swung around 180 degrees.

Under normal circumstances a boat is pushed forward by waves rather than throttled by them, but for *Climate Action Now*, being held in place by the fallen mast, the storm-driven waves became battering rams. "The waves and wind were pushing the mast up onto the deck of the boat," Lisa explains. "Every approaching wave would grab the sails and the rigging and lines that were in the water and shove it all up onto the deck and the next wave would drag it off again. The boat was converted into a rudimentary seesaw, jolting back and forth, over and over. Immediately, my brain clicked into fight-or-flight response and all of my thoughts went to freeing the mast. Otherwise, one of those waves was going to push the mast through the hull of the boat, pierce the side of it, and sink her."

Lisa was in the grips of a massive storm, about 1,000 nautical miles from land, with no ship traffic near. She was remote, and she was alone. She would later discover that the closest ship was over 600 nautical miles away. "If I lost the boat that far south, there was no second chance, even if I jumped in a life raft with my survival suit, the chances of recovery were so slim for any ship to even find me, let alone find me alive if

I hadn't succumbed to exposure. So I had to free the mast at all costs."

Through the inky darkness of an angry night, Lisa set about trying to save her boat. She had to free the destroyed mast. Freeing a mast is a delicate procedure in calm conditions, but in the frenzy of a storm, as a boat pitches and rolls with waves washing across its deck, it would prove a life-threatening task.

To release the mast Lisa needed to uncouple the rigging. To do this she needed to disengage a split-pin at the connection point at several locations. "I tried to hammer them out with my screwdriver and my hammer and it just wasn't working," she recalls. "I was shaking so bad, I couldn't aim right with the hammer and I kept smashing my left hand. My whole hand ballooned up as I had likely broken a few bones."

The storm raged on as Lisa kept hammering. She eventually managed to separate the backstay and the inner forestay from the rigging and was left with the side stays and the forward piece of rigging of the forestay to detach. She needed to separate the forestay next but faced a difficult quandary. "I realized that I couldn't get access to that piece of rigging wire without putting my arm directly underneath the broken mast and, once the mast released, it would collapse and break my arm," she explains. "The alternative was to jump over the bow rail and sit down on my bowsprit (the horizontal pole-like protuberance extending forward from the vessel's prow) and release it from there. Now, I was in 20- to 25-foot [6- to 8-meter] breaking waves, and every 30 seconds I am getting completely engulfed by white water. To climb out there, I had a very slim shot of success. I remember being on my hands and knees on deck thinking there's got to be another way." There wasn't.

"It was madness and I was so not wanting to go out there," she continues. "I just stared and stared as all the scenarios played out in my mind and none of them had a good ending. As I was kneeling frozen on the bow, another rope snapped that was holding the mast above the deck. I was running out of time and I didn't have a choice. It was to go out on that bowsprit and free the rigging or lose the boat. Losing the boat was not an option."

Lisa Blair on deck of her yacht *Climate Action Now*   Courtesy of Lisa Blair. Photo credit Mark Harkup

Lisa crawled out on the end of the bowsprit and sat down. A huge wave washed over her and the boat rolled wildly. "My legs were clamped so hard and I was gripping the remaining bit of railing with a death grip as I held on." She needed to time her work with the gaps in the waves, letting go everything and hammering for all she's worth when she was in the trough of a wave and hanging on when the next one approached. "I remember looking to the left at the waves and seeing only darkness, but there was just enough difference in color for me to make out the waves," she explains. "They were well above me, the height of your average tree. Just towering over me and I just kept thinking

'Oh crap, oh crap, this is so not good, oh crap, oh crap.'" She cycled through her hands-on-again-hands-off-again rodeo ride until the split-pin finally popped loose. She scrambled back on deck amazed she had made it through alive. She made quick work of the side stays and watched her mast slip beneath the ocean surface. She had saved the boat and herself.

* * *

Lisa was still shaking violently from the cold and adrenaline and quickly retreated to the cabin in an attempt to get warm. It would take several hours wrapped in her sleeping bag before the shaking would ease and her body temperature would rise. The barometer was finally rising too, and it was only then that she realized what a close call she'd endured. She had survived, but just barely. After patching holes and making some basic repairs, Lisa began the demoralizing voyage north to land. "I had to make the call to abandon the record and put the motor on and start motoring up to Cape Town." She says. "I was devastated. I was happy to have lived and survived the night, but I was also completely gutted because it meant three and a half years of hard work down the drain."

A large Chinese container ship had been rerouted south to meet her. The idea was that the boats would rendezvous, and the container ship would transfer her some additional fuel, as her reserves were inadequate to motor the 1,000-nautical-mile journey to South Africa. It would take the ship three days to reach her because of the high seas. "The seas were so big for them that they had to travel at six knots—half the usual speed of a container ship," Lisa explains, "They had to slow down so much. A big container ship can get caught on the peak of a wave with the middle of the ship on the peak and then the bow and stern aren't supported and gravity takes over and it can literally snap the ship in half. The container ship pilots were concerned that this could happen because of how big the seas were."

When they rendezvoused, Lisa was faced with the challenging task of transferring the fuel and a captain on the container ship who wasn't sure how to do it. "They were literally going to try to tie me up alongside like we were at a fuel dock and fill my tank with this bowser line." She explains. "Now the side of the ship is 30 meters (100 feet) high, so gravity alone with that bowser line would have flooded my boat with diesel simply because of gravity pulling that fuel down. We were still in 6-meter swell with 25-knot winds. They were pitching and rolling port and starboard. They said come along side and tie up. I said 'No way. I'm not tying up! It's too dangerous!'"

The container ship measured 200 meters (600 feet) in length and weighed over 86,000 tons. It was the size of a 70-story skyscraper on its side, clad in cold steel, bouncing around wildly in the ocean. It was a case of the elephant and the mouse for the size of her small fiberglass sailboat to the giant container ship. One misstep, and she would be sunk.

"What ended up happening was a bit of a standoff," she says. "After six hours, they convinced me to take one line from the stern of their ship to the bow of my boat, and the intention was I would hold my boat in reverse from off the corner of the ship and they would pass the jerry cans down that single line. So I took the line on and the next minute I look up there are 10 blokes untying me from the ship and then they start dragging me up the side of the ship to the starboard side where their fenders are. They were going to tie me off. Within seconds the ship drifted on top of me and I had this 86,000-ton ship rolling and rocking and smashing into my boat. They would roll toward me and crush the side of the boat, then roll away and then roll back on top of me again."

The crew of the container ship had no idea what was happening. They were likely more accustomed to tugboats hammering into the side of their hull and had no understanding of the fragility of Lisa's craft. "I looked up and they were taking photos. They still hadn't grasped the concept they were sinking my boat! I ran forward and threw off their line from the bow of my boat and then ran back and went hard in reverse, and I ended up bouncing my way down the side of this container ship as we came in contact. There was this one incredible moment where the back corner of the ship lifted up on the peak of a wave and rolled away from me, and I turned hard away from the ship, and the whole bow of my boat went under the back corner of the container ship, and they rolled back down and crashed into the water, and I seriously thought I was going to lose the first two meters of my boat. I was 15 centimetres clear somehow."

Lisa was terrified and overwhelmed. She now had a three-meter-long crack down the side of her boat from the collision. The Maritime Rescue Coordination Centre in Cape Town, whom she had been in continuous contact with, was now pressuring her to abandon ship and take rescue from the container ship. "They said in no uncertain terms that if I don't take this rescue now, they won't be sending any further aid to me," she says. "At this point you have to understand, from a woman's point of view in a man's industry, that if I had taken that rescue, I feel I would never have had any ability to ever again do another solo trip on a boat at this competitive level. It's a catch-22 with this marine industry, I feel it is so judgmental of women, and so for my own future, I kept going. I wasn't ready to quit myself, and I truly believed that my boat could make it. I needed another chance."

Eventually the captain of the container ship lowered the fuel in containers into the sea, as per Lisa's request, where she could collect them safely and head north on her way. She would jerry-rig her boom to act as a mast and would limp into Cape Town worn out but not beaten. She would spend two months in South Africa and restart her journey to a chorus of naysayers saying she had no business heading back out again. "Even the experienced sailors were messaging me," she says. "So I said to them, I'm comfortable continuing based on the grounds of my research and the risks I've assessed. Where's the data saying it's not possible to sail those conditions? Tell me where that data is? And nobody could give me any data."

Winter had now descended on the Southern Ocean, and with it came colder weather, bigger waves, and hurricane-sized storms. After the monumental challenges and disappointments of the previous months, any regular person would have called it quits, but not Lisa. In her mind she had started something, and she was going to finish it. She was not to be deterred. On June 12, 2017, Lisa set sail from Cape Town, South Africa, and headed due south to rejoin her circumnavigation route at the point of her dismasting. She knew full well what horrors might await her out there, yet she chose to continue anyhow. What special something kept her going? What made Lisa so resilient?

Building Resilience: Preparing for the Worst

Facing setbacks is part of being human. Some people, like Lisa Blair, put themselves in situations where significant setbacks and failures seem to be inevitable. To the outsider, deciding to sail around Antarctica, through some of the most dangerous waters on the planet, seems fraught with disaster. But from Lisa's perspective, it's not the risk of failing that was the scary part but rather the risk of not having tried. "If you try and push yourself, and if you can start something and succeed, what else are you capable of?" Lisa openly says when we speak. "After I finish a trip, I always ask myself, so 'what else can you achieve? What else are you capable of?' And from that line of questioning, I ended up doing one of the hardest things in the world."

Lisa is quick to point out that she is an ordinary person pushing herself to achieve the extraordinary. She believes we are all capable of achieving what we want if we really want it badly enough. "I'm a massive believer in that I'm no one special," she says. "Yes, I've gone and done some amazing things, but I'm 5 feet 2 inches, 80 kilograms, I'm not a fit Amazonian warrior, I'm just me. I think so many people underestimate what they're capable of because they haven't started on a journey of finding out who they are. They've settled in their life. One of the biggest things I try to get across is you can do it. You have to want to do it. And want it enough to do it. Anyone can do it. Everyone is physically capable. But you have to want it enough."

Lisa Blair personifies resilience in her drive to complete what she puts her mind to, regardless of the setbacks she faces. Her ability to face her own mortality during her dismasting and to have the mental wherewithal to come through it is inspirational. But for her then to return to the exact same spot of her undoing and restart her journey is truly extraordinary. It speaks volumes to her remarkable capacity for resilience. What is it about Lisa that allows her to adapt so well in the face of adversity? How was she able to bounce back from the brink of despair, learn and grow, and then go on to ultimately succeed? Let's take a closer look.

Resilience is a difficult capacity to measure because it only exhibits itself when it's needed. As the Russian-American writer and psychologist Maria Konnikova writes in her article "How People Learn to Become Resilient" for the *New Yorker,*

"Whether you can be said to have [resilience] or not largely depends not on any particular psychological test but on the way your life unfolds. If you are lucky enough to never experience any sort of adversity, we won't know how resilient you are. It's only when you're faced with obstacles, stress, and other environmental threats that resilience, or the lack of it, emerges. Do you succumb or do you surmount?"[1]

The good thing is that resilience is not a genetic trait but rather a skill that can be developed over time. When resilience is developed, we are better able to face those moments of adversity when they arise and deal with them. By practicing the skills of resilience, you will develop a stronger capacity for it, and just like with a muscle, your capacity for resilience will become stronger with this practice.

Developmental psychologist Emmy Werner undertook a 40-year longitudinal study of 698 infants on the Hawaiian island of Kauai with the intent of understanding how environmental and reproductive risk factors affect the outcomes of children relative to those who have not experienced such challenges. The study looked at the entire birth cohort for the island for the year 1955 and presented a unique opportunity to look at and understand how resilience affected the children's outcomes in a relatively insulated environment.[2] Over the course of the study, she discovered that one third of the high-risk children, despite their challenges, showed high degrees of resilience and went on to become caring productive adults. She and fellow researchers were able to identify that these children possessed protective factors that helped them navigate the difficulties they faced and they had developed skills and strategies to improve their resilience.[3]

What Werner also discovered was that resilience would transform over time depending on the circumstances. "Some children were especially unlucky: they experienced multiple strong stressors (such as being born prematurely, having an unstable household, or a mentally ill mother) at vulnerable points and their resilience evaporated. Resilience, she explained, is like a constant calculation: Which side of the equation weighs more, the resilience or the stressors? The stressors can become so intense that resilience is overwhelmed. Most people, in short, have a breaking point. On the flip side, some people who weren't resilient when they were younger somehow learned the skills of resilience. They overcame adversity later in life and went on to flourish as much as those who'd been resilient their entire lives. This, of course, raises the question of how resilience might be learned."[4]

Looking at Lisa's story to help answer this question, believing you are capable of doing what you want to do is the first critical step in learning to become resilient. Whatever it is you want to do may seem impossible at first, but if you truly believe you are capable of doing it and you are willing to take the necessary steps to achieve it, then you can do it.

Taking the necessary steps to build resilience, as Lisa demonstrates, means becoming thoroughly prepared, and it is through this preparation that your capability manifests. "I think one of the biggest lessons I learned is I wouldn't have survived the dismasting if I didn't have the right preparation. It was mental and physical preparation. It was having the right tools onboard, but it was also having spent the time thinking about all possible emergencies before I left, instead of freaking out about it when I was out there. With a journey like this, preparation is so important because if you cut any corners, you're not going to succeed. Preparation is the vital part of success. If you've prepped well, you've eliminated the risk through your preparation."

But real preparation comes at the cost of time and effort, and this was something that Lisa was willing to pay for. Preparation for her began three and a half years before she reached the start line of her Antarctic adventure. She wanted to build capacity as an open ocean sailor and sought about finding the best way to do it quickly. She learned about the amateur Clipper Round the World yacht race, founded by sailor Robert Knox-Johnston, where 16 to 18 amateur crew members are teamed up with an experienced skipper and race around the world. For a fee of 80,000 Australian dollars, participants race around the world for a year. It was exactly what she was looking for. But she didn't have the money to do it.

"I was working in the mall making 20 bucks an hour," she says. "I could never earn that sort of money. It took me two months to come to terms that it may not be possible for me to raise that kind of money. No one in my family had ever done anything like that before. We never fundraised; we had never done anything of that scale before. My family thought it was a massive long shot, but I ended up committing to the race."

Over the next year Lisa would do everything in her power to raise the funds. "I cycled my bike 1,300 kilometers from Sydney to the Sunshine Coast," she explains. "I rode 100 kilometers per day, and each night I would walk around the local restaurants and pubs and sell raffle tickets for a diamond ring that we had donated to the trip." She saved and she hustled and did everything she could do to put money away. The deadline approached, and her father took out a mortgage against their family home to add to the pot, yet she was still 2,000 Australian dollars short with only two weeks to go. In a desperate final effort, she went to the local newspaper on the Sunshine Coast and asked them to run a story about her dilemma. An American expat living in China who had holidayed on the Sunshine Coast was, by chance, perusing the *Sunshine Coast Daily* online that day. He read the article and donated the final 2,000 dollars that night. Tenacity, belief, and a little bit of luck paid off.

"I spent a year racing this boat around the world and just trying to maximize my learning," she explains. "By the end of the year when we had finished the circumnavigation I had more than enough experience to be a skipper, and I was comfortable in all sorts of conditions and disasters, and I had this newfound confidence in my sailing. And when I got back from that trip, I remember thinking to myself what I was now capable of."

Lisa Blair wrestles with a broken mast on her yacht *Climate Action Now*   *Courtesy of Lisa Blair*

Whenever we face a new challenge in our lives, whether it be taking on a new role as a leader, reinventing ourselves professionally, or even sailing around Antarctica solo, we want to succeed. But with any new challenge come setbacks and with these setbacks comes the capacity to be thrown off track. To prevent this, we need to prepare ourselves. Being prepared for worst-case scenarios is something we all need to do to be at our resilient best and is something Lisa did exceptionally well for her expedition.

"For Antarctica I set the goal of getting to the start, and I recognized that that would be one of the hardest parts of the trip and it was," she says. "I would visualize the worst-case scenarios, I visualized what it would be like if I dismasted, if I got rolled over by a wave, what would happen if I lost my keel, what would happen if I lost my rudder, what would happen if I got injured?"

Lisa set up if-then scenario plans—"if something bad happens, then this is how I will respond"—and then moved on without dwelling on them. She reduced her overall stress by planning what she would do if something went wrong rather than simply hoping it wouldn't. Planning meant moving forward for her, hoping meant standing still.

Being under stress takes an emotional toll on us that can easily build to chronic levels if we don't allow time for recovery. Stress produces chemicals in our blood called glucocorticoids.[5] These chemicals reduce the symptoms of post-traumatic stress disorder (PTSD) and anxiety and are critical for recovery and resilience, but unfortunately, chronic stress inhibits the processing of these chemicals and results in acute stress without a method of recovery. This oftentimes leads to negative lifestyle adaptations like eating too much, drinking, smoking, and sleeping less. When the wear and tear on the body accumulated from repeated stress reaches a tipping point, it results in a physiological response called allostatic overload.[6] Think of an acutely stressed brain like that of a sore muscle after too much use. It needs recovery time to bounce back, or it will begin to deteriorate. Planning and preparing for those moments of recovery when you are aware of an acute stressor or chronic stressor coming your way can help you proactively build your resilience.

On May 1, 2015, Sheryl Sandberg's life would change forever with the sudden death of her husband, Dave Goldberg.

Sandberg, the chief operating officer for Facebook, was so over-come with grief that at the time she could not imagine herself ever feeling joy again. At a particularly dark point in her suffer-ing, she reached out to her friend Adam Grant, a psychology professor at University of Pennsylvania, and asked for help. Grant would console Sandberg and explain that what she was feeling was a perfectly normal response and that grief needed time to run its course.

What started out as comforting words of advice from a friend soon blossomed into a writing partnership that chronicled Sand-berg's difficult recovery back from heartache. *Option B: Facing Adversity, Building Resilience, and Finding Joy* openly discusses Sandberg's journey back from intense grief and explores the idea that one can learn and grow from acute trauma. The book also investigates how pretraumatic growth, the concept that appreci-ating life and bolstering one's ability to have gratitude without experiencing trauma (knowing that it is inevitable at some point) will enhance one's overall resilience. The two authors suggest that to be at our resilient-best we should all practice the emo-tional fitness regime of appreciating the little things that make life great in order to counteract stress.[7]

Lisa Blair undertook her own emotional fitness regime before her Antarctic journey by observing others on their emotional roller-coaster ride of self-reflection. "When I did the Clipper Round the World yacht race, we had 'leggers' [individuals who joined the sailing crew on one leg, but not the entire trip] come on during sections. I had already done my first major crossing at 22 and had that emotional experience before that trip. I had done my internal processing and decided who I wanted to be and just went and became that person. I watched so many peo-ple go through that journey in 30 days. It was interesting to see what happened to people. You have so much time on the water to think about yourself and to process life decisions, it was a moment when so many people learned about themselves."

What Lisa understood was that what you learn about yourself in those moments of introspection, what is important in your life, the appreciation of what you have and what you have achieved, is critical to building your resilience.

Build Your Crew: Strong Relationships

Social connectedness is one of the key attributes of resilient people. Studies suggest strong social relationships reduce both psychological and physiological stress. In a study in the *Journal of Nutrition, Health & Aging*, researcher R. M. Guimarães reported that "socially connected individuals displayed less systolic and diastolic blood pressure reactivity on days characterized by high negative emotional arousal (stress). Those high in social connectedness showed greater ability to inhibit the detrimental impact of negative emotion on subsequent cardiovascular responses."[8] In other words, socially connected people were less stressed, showed less physiological deterioration from that stress, and were ultimately more resilient overall. But there should be little surprise in this. As human beings we're social creatures through and through, and our social connectedness naturally bolsters our capacity to deal with adversity and setback. Lisa had strong social connections and without them, she would never have succeeded.

Lisa's family was always there when she needed them with her mom being her pillar of support. "Having mum around was a massive help to me mentally and physically to keep me grounded and focused," she says. Having someone in your corner who believes in your dream or your goal as much as you do allows you to get reprogrammed mentally or reset when things don't go well.

When Lisa sailed south to rejoin the position where she dismasted two months earlier, she discovered the seas had taken a turn for the worse. It was winter now in the Southern Ocean, and the intensity and frequency of storms had increased. "I was trying to push across these storms, they were coming in every other day and each storm was the size of a hurricane," she explains. "As they were coming across, pushing this massive swell, and the forecast during summer was 8 to 10 meters [25 to 30 feet] during a storm, whereas in winter, the forecast was showing 15 meters [50 feet] in the middle of a storm. Five extra meters!"

After five days of struggle, she was exhausted and was still a long way from her dismasting point. She had pushed for three-and-a-half years just to get to the start of her journey. She had endured 72 brutal days at sea before she was dismasted. She had survived the dismasting by the skin of her teeth and limped to land for repairs. She then spent two months desperately putting her boat back together while fending off the vitriol of trolls and naysayers who were telling her she was crazy. She soldiered on and, through it all, made it as far as she had, but now she reached her breaking point. "I was spiralling downward," she recalls. "I was starting to get quite terrified, because I built it up in my head as all these problems. I remember making the decision five days in to turn around and go back to South Africa and being absolutely shattered. I was in tears, constantly. I couldn't keep myself together for any amount of time. I called my mum up and said, 'I'm going back. It's too dangerous. I'm heading back to South Africa.'"

Lisa's mom provided the support she needed, exactly when she needed it. "In that call she said, 'If you really think it's a safety problem, if it's too dangerous, turn back,'" she recalls. "'We'll find a way and make it work. But just imagine this. Imagine you're 72 days into your record, you're four weeks from home, you're one day ahead of the men's record, and you're on the final stretch and you're feeling like this and you're sailing in conditions like this. In that moment, would these conditions be enough to make you quit?'"

Lisa's mom was pivotal in shaking her out of her emotional response to the situation and returned her to a logical thinking process. "I let those people get into my head and cause me to doubt myself because I was so tired and so close to land. I had so much negative messaging come through. So after that discussion with Mum, I decided to continue."

A wet and exhausted Lisa Blair celebrates rounding Cape Horn on her yacht
Climate Action Now   *Courtesy of Lisa Blair*

Strong relationships like the one Lisa demonstrates with her mother help buffer the emotional response to challenge and failure that we all experience, yet so many of us "go it alone," thinking resilience needs to be built internally.

Oftentimes, the well-being and stress levels of employees are used as indicators of resilience within an organization, and as a result, it is in these areas that companies make interventions to help build resilience. But by digging deeper we realize there is more to it. Having a strong, collaborative network to get through tough times or unexpected challenges builds a greater sense of resilience. Seeking support from managers, getting feedback and input, and asking for help are all elements that help build resilience within people in an organization.[9]

Realistic Optimism

Lisa kept clawing south for another five days to reach her dismasting position and then, at long last, turned "left" and continued on her journey to Australia. "The thing that happened that was really interesting, the minute I started heading back to Oz, everything became a lot easier," she says with an air of amazement in her voice. "Storms weren't as aggressive, traveling with the swell versus against it, the swells didn't hit me as badly, I wasn't getting rolled or knocked down as badly. And also, mentally, I knew I was doing it, so my whole attitude changed. I became much more positive, buoyant, and energetic."

After 183 days, Lisa Blair sailed back into Albany in Western Australia and crossed her track below 45 degrees south and completed her circumnavigation of the Southern Ocean. Deducting the time lost to her dismasting and repairs in South Africa, she would have completed the journey in 103 days, one day slower than the men's record. Had she not had to sail the final section in winter, she would have gone faster and beaten the men's record outright. "I felt disappointed that I wasn't able to beat the record, but in the end, I didn't give up and I didn't quit or become one of those people who says, 'oh this is too hard' and walks away. I'm incredibly proud of what I accomplished."

In a 2011 *Harvard Business Review* article, "Building Resilience," author and director of the Positive Psychology Center at the University of Pennsylvania, Martin Seligman suggests that creating a positive narrative for ourselves is a critical part of being resilient. "We discovered that people who don't give up have a habit of interpreting setbacks as temporary, local, and changeable. Using self-talk including, 'It's going away quickly; it's just this one situation, and I can do something about it' can really help. It suggests how we might immunize people against learned helplessness, against depression and anxiety, and against giving up after failure: by teaching them to think like optimists."[10]

Being resilient requires giving ourselves a "cognitive intervention" and countering defeatist thinking with an optimistic attitude.[11] Building up our own positive stories into libraries in our heads allows us to face difficulty or the constant stressors of life. Because resilience is a dynamic process, not a point-in-time action, the internal dialogue you have with yourself and the attitude you take makes a difference in your ability to recover quickly from the setbacks you have and the emotional tolls they take.

There is also a misconception portrayed that resilience is only built through these "tough" endeavors. However, according to Shawn Achor and Michelle Geilan of the Institute for Applied Positive Research, in their 2016 *Harvard Business Review* article "Resilience Is About How You Recharge, Not About How You Endure," the recharge and learning process of giving yourself time to stop, recover, and learn, and then to try again, believing that you can accomplish what you are setting out to do, is just as important.[12] These recovery times reduce allostatic load—the elevated endocrine and neural responses to chronic stress. Two of the most popular ways to promote ongoing recovery are the practices of meditation and journaling on gratitude, each of which can enhance the emotional regulation that allows you to put challenges into perspective and bounce back from moments where your resilience is taxed. Both put you into an optimistic mind frame as well.

Maintaining a sense of realistic optimism is important from a biological standpoint as well. According to Judith and Richard Glazer, who wrote *The Neurochemistry of Positive Conversation,* our biochemistry changes when we are faced with criticism. When we are criticized, feel rejection or fear, our bodies produce "higher levels of cortisol, a hormone that shuts down the thinking center of our brains and activates conflict aversion and protection behaviors. We become more reactive and sensitive." Cortisol lasts a long time in our systems, lasting for sometimes 26 hours or more, "imprinting the (negative) interactions on our memories and magnifying the impact they have on our future behaviour." The longer we ruminate about our fears and challenges, the longer the impact. There was little doubt that the incessant rant of naysayers questioning her decision to head back out on her journey spiked Lisa's cortisol levels and her viewing her situation through a negative lens. The support Lisa received from her mother extricated her from it and allowed a sense of realistic optimism to seep back in. The boost of positivity she gained from this interaction would also spark a chemical reaction in her body, but its effect would be far less robust. When we get support from others, we get a boost of oxytocin in our systems. It makes us feel positive, connected, and more trusting, but unfortunately this neurotransmitter and hormone metabolizes much faster than cortisol and its effects are less intense and long-lasting. For Lisa and for all of us, redoubling our efforts to be optimistic and positive in the face of challenge is not only sage advice from a rational point of view, but is imperative from a biochemical perspective as well.

"It wasn't just one adventure or just one moment in time that sparked the idea for the Antarctic circumnavigation," says Lisa. "It was by doing a series of other adventures that I started to gain the experience and started to realize that we are far more capable than we realize."

"My mom's partner had all these books on sailing and he let me read them," she continues. "They were all solo sailing books. Kay Coddy, Robert Knox Johnson, Jessie Martin, Peter Grass. As I would read them, I'd get more inclined to go ocean sailing and solo sailing. What struck me about their stories was that they were just normal people, they didn't have a separate set of super skills . . . , they weren't paragons of fitness, they were just average people, and for me it meant that potentially achievable down the track."

Reading these books stimulated Lisa to write her own stories and to journal about her experiences. Her journal became a place to reflect on the events of her trip, allowing her to process the emotional and challenging events in a regulated way, reviewing her responses and reactions to events with her spirit of optimism.

The modern video gaming industry, which you might think, on the surface, is literally "all fun and games," deals with its own emotional challenges on a regular basis. Game developers are highly competitive in their quest to gain market share in what's an 81-billion-dollar industry with fickle consumers and high expectations. Internally, production deadlines are driven hard with unchangeable release dates, big publicity, and high pressure. Most of the larger game development companies are on two-plus year cycles in which they create and produce a single game with little idea on how it will be received by the consumer. When a game proves not to be a big hit in the marketplace, these companies either scramble to make edits and communicate, or accept failure, sell at a massive discount, and try to bounce back and be creative again.

In 2018 Electronic Arts (EA), the developer responsible for games including *The Sims*, *Madden NFL*, and *FIFA* soccer, was faced with a profound setback that transcended their usual competitive challenges. On August 26, in Jacksonville Landing, Florida, two players were shot and killed and nine others were injured in a mass shooting by another player during a tournament where EA's popular *Madden NFL* video game was the focal point.[13] Although the event itself was not organized in any way by EA, the company nonetheless stepped up to support the families of the two victims, Taylor Robertson and Eli Clayton. The organization grieved as if these players were part of their team and demonstrated clearly that they were deeply impacted by the tragedy. Andrew Wilson, EA's CEO, flew to Florida to meet with employees and families to provide emotional support. The company offered counseling and specifically recognized the victims, sharing their gaming stories and creating a community to grieve and heal. EA set up a foundation that eventually raised 1.2 million dollars for the families of these victims. Internally, EA immediately canceled all upcoming events to reassess security protocols and to scenario plan for future events so focus would be on the safety of players, employees, and fans. The company demonstrated resilience by applying the lessons learned from the event and committing to preventing further tragedies from happening, not just at tournaments, but at any large public gathering where the EA community was present. In the year following the shooting, the company hasn't tried to distance itself from the event and its emotional impact, but rather uses it as a reminder to be steadfast in their vision and continue to tell stories and create events, "to inspire the world to play." EA's resilience as a company allowed it to move forward through tragedy and demonstrate to the world that it is committed to both its people and to the entire gaming community at large.

Building Your Resilience

We can learn a lot from Lisa's tough-as-nails approach to her accomplishments. Her modesty is apparent from the stories she tells, facing some of the most difficult adventures on earth, but in her stories, there are lessons for us to consider. We may not be forced to fight for our lives on the Southern Ocean, but there are three ways we can integrate Lisa's hardiness into our own lives:

1. **Prepare for worst-case scenarios.** By using all of her technical capability and prior experience, Lisa knew how to tap into her toolkit, both practically and emotionally, when she needed to. She built much of her practical sailing experience by undertaking the Clipper Round the World yacht race, and through it she got a crash course on the skills she would need to be a solo skipper. The yearlong sailing journey functioned as an internship on the water and allowed her a safe environment to practice her skills and respond to problems. Lisa built her emotional skills by mentally preparing for her journey by visualizing a myriad of scenarios that could go wrong and preparing for them with "if-then" plans before she set sail. This allowed her to practice and better understand how she would emotionally respond when

something bad actually did happen. Often the fear of the unknown is more difficult than actually dealing with a problem you have already prepared for mentally. By practicing her skills and building her toolkit over time, Lisa was able to build her capacity for resilience and be at her best when things were at their worst.

In the work you do, how often are you doing this level of preplanning? Next time before you make an important decision, give a presentation, or get in front of a customer, think about what the worst-case scenario could be if everything went sideways. With this in mind, plan a response and file it away. By doing this you're minimizing the surprise you feel when something does go wrong and your helping regulate your emotional response to it, if and when it does happen.

2. **Sustain strong relationships.** Building resilience requires us to go through hard times, but it's not something that we have to do alone. Strong relationships help buoy us and keep our spirits up. They buffer our emotional response to failure, give us perspective when it's lacking, and have the power to call us out with some tough love, just like Lisa's mother demonstrated, when we need it most. We fare much better if we build and sustain strong relationships—we know this intuitively and the science backs us up. In the case of EA, they banded together as an organization, led by their CEO, to work through tragedy and heal. Building strong personal relationships with your team when times are good can buoy you when things get tough—even when they are at their worst.

3. **Create stories with a sense of realistic optimism.** Lisa didn't waste any time dwelling on her failure when she had a setback. She acknowledged and understood her

problem and continued to be proactive and focused on finding solutions for it. Lisa's strong belief in her capabilities, while accurately assessing the challenges she faced, kept her going and pushing forward. As someone who is positive by nature, Lisa didn't discount the real problems at hand but understood how to reduce the emotional aspects of failure and got constructive in her thinking.

This optimism and sense of belief keeps Lisa going. In fact, she is planning her next adventure to head back out on the Southern Ocean and take another crack at what she attempted. Lisa has some unfinished business at hand. "I would like to go and do Antarctica again nonstop and get the record," she says. "If I go back the second time around, it will be battling my demons from the dismasting, but also closing that loop and succeeding and knowing that I can, giving me more faith in my own abilities."

And her abilities are only building as are her optimism and resilience. "I'm also looking at going around the Arctic nonstop, which is a very interesting project," she says. "I think it's a step up from Antarctica because I'd be around ice consistently. It would be an amazing follow-on from that trip. Dealing with all those issues gets me excited about this project. Finding out the risks and how I should negate them or work around them."

There's little doubt she will find lots of risk and challenge on this voyage. In 2013, I (author Kevin) was a member of a four-man team that attempted to row across the Northwest Passage in a custom-designed ocean rowing boat. We were out there making a statement about the profound changes happening in the Arctic. The journey was the most challenging adventure of my life and was rife with struggle and uncertainty. But this is the type of environment in which Lisa Blair thrives, and there's little doubt she's up to the challenge and has the robust resilience to pull it off.

CHAPTER 7

Personal Sustainability

Building Balance

"How do you keep going? Why don't you quit?"

Kevin Vallely was at his wit's end when he read the email message. He was sitting in his tent in the middle of Antarctica, halfway through his ski to the South Pole when the message appeared on his screen. It caught him completely off-guard. Kevin was part of a three-man Canadian team attempting to break the world record for the fastest unsupported ski traverse from the edge of the Antarctic continent to the geographic South Pole, a brutal 660-mile journey across one of the harshest environments on the planet. And Kevin was completely exhausted.

It was three days before Christmas, and Kevin would be spending the holiday away from his two young daughters for the first time. Every time he'd speak to them on the satellite phone, they'd ask when he'd be home, and each time, attempting to conceal his dejection, he'd say in as upbeat a voice as possible, "As soon as I can, sweetie, as soon as I can!" "It was heartbreaking," he says. "I wanted to be back with them so badly. They were really young and had no real understanding what I was doing other than I wouldn't be there for Christmas. It was really hard!"

Adding to his emotional angst was his physical exhaustion. "We were pulling everything we needed to survive with us in our sleds," he says. "It was like pulling a refrigerator that weighed more than 250 pounds. Additionally, I was the photographer and videographer for the expedition and found myself routinely chasing after my two teammates who were more focused on maintaining their fast pace than waiting for me to repack my camera gear. It was brutal!" Kevin was at his physical and mental limit when he read that email.

As part of their expedition, the team had over 10,000 schoolkids from across North America following them, and thanks to satellite technology they were able to communicate with the students. "They'd email us countless questions each day," he said. "And each evening we'd try to answer as many as we could. It was something our team really enjoyed." Most questions were simple and easy to answer.

Kevin Vallely traversing the glare ice of Lake Baikal, Siberia, on his record-breaking crossing

Courtesy of Kevin Vallely

SANDRA: "Are you cold?"

KEVIN: "Well, Sandra, most of the time. It's really cold and windy here. In fact, Antarctica is the coldest continent on earth. Temperatures have been recorded here as low as –129.3°F or –189.6°C!"

JOHNNY: "What do you eat?"

KEVIN: "We're on a crazy diet. We need to eat upward of 8,000 calories a day just to survive! We're eating foods like deep-fried bacon and chunks of butter the size of a billiard ball! How would you like to eat that, Johnny?"

GEOFF: "What animals do you see?"

KEVIN: "There's no life out here at all, Geoff! There is lots of life on the perimeter of the continent, where it meets the ocean, but up here, on the polar plateau, there's nothing. The only living thing is a half-inch insect that exists on a distant mountain range in Antarctica. It survives on bacteria. But other than that little bug, it's just us. And good thing, too, as we haven't been out of our same clothing since we arrived on the continent, and we would scare off any living creatures! ☺"

And then Kevin read the question, "How do you keep going? Why don't you quit?"

The question was from a young offender named Sammy, incarcerated at the Riverside Resolve detention center in Chicago. Sammy was a strike two offender, meaning if this kid made one more mistake, he was headed to adult court and adult prison. Sammy was a kid on the fringe, and Kevin knew it. Sammy's question stopped him cold. Kevin couldn't answer him. It was clear his question meant a lot more to him than simply trying to understand how Kevin kept skiing. He was reaching out to him because of his own struggles. But what Sammy didn't know was that Kevin's journey to the South Pole hadn't started a couple weeks earlier on the Ronne Ice Shelf, but started on a stormy wintery night 35 years earlier in Montreal, Canada, when he was a young boy. Here he was sitting in his tent asking himself the very same thing, and then this.

It was a Friday night in Montreal, Canada, during the winter of 1974, when Kevin and his brother Michael joined their parents for an evening out, shopping in the center of town. It was a cold and blustery night, and the family elected to stay inside and browse the big department stores rather than brave the ice and snow on St. Catherine's Street. Why Kevin and Michael became separated from their parents is lost on him now, but they were young boys likely acting their age. It was closing time at the store, and an overzealous security guard decided to kick them out rather than help them find their parents. Kevin was ten years old, and his brother was six.

"I remember that moment like it was yesterday," recalls Kevin. "We were firmly ushered out of the department store onto a busy street and left there. It was snowing heavily at the time. I remember all the people and the cars, and I felt so scared. I didn't know what to do. Then my brother started to cry. 'I want Mommy! I want to go home,' he said."

The two youngsters weren't dressed for the frigid weather, having come to town by bus, and they had no money. Their parents were nowhere to be seen. "I remember this overwhelming feeling of anxiety and uncertainty of not knowing what to do, but knowing it was completely up to me to do it," recalls Kevin. "I took my brother by the hand and said, 'I'll get us home,' and I started walking." Looking back on it now, Kevin realizes, "I had no idea where I was going. I didn't know where home was, but the walking warmed us and eased our minds." His brother trusted him, and Kevin did his best to disguise his uncertainty.

"I walked south at first," he says. "I know this now because of the building I recognized—the Chateau Champlain. Our family called it the cheese grater because it was tall and slim with semicircular windows and looked like a cheese grater. I knew immediately that was the wrong way, and I turned around and headed in the other direction."

He looked for anything he would recognize but nothing was familiar. He passed St. Catherine's Street and de Maisonneuve Street, but at the time, the names would have been meaningless to him. "Then I saw Sherbrooke Street," he recalls. He recognized that name. He knew he lived close to a Sherbrooke Street. "Maybe if I follow this street, I'll find home," he says. "And that's what I did."

It was near midnight when the familiar sites of our neighborhood began to appear through the veil of the winter storm. Kevin and his brother passed Murray Hill Park, a local sledding area they would frequent, and a short time later saw the familiar sights of home and a waiting patrol car in front of their apartment building. "It's funny looking back on it now," says Kevin. "But the first thing I remember thinking was, 'Why is there a police car in front of my building? I wonder what's wrong?'"

The brothers were welcomed with the reassuring embrace of very relieved parents. "I remember my mom being so happy to see us," says Kevin. "I had thought we had done something wrong, but she was so proud of us. She couldn't believe I got us home safely."

The feeling of that moment, of fear blanketed in accomplishment, has stayed with Kevin his whole life. It was one of the scariest moments he had experienced as a child, but it was also one of the most empowering. "In a few short hours, I was forced to rethink what was possible for me," he says. "Responsibility, self-reliance, inspiration, all rolled into one."

This was Kevin's first taste of adventure, and it wasn't long after this that he began to dream of skiing to the South Pole. "It's kind of nuts, looking back," he says, "I was an urban, inner-city kid who knew nothing of outdoor adventure, but that didn't matter one iota to me, I had this crazy dream. I wanted to ski to the South Pole." He points to this experience as to why he became an explorer.

As life moved forward, Kevin's dream to ski to the South Pole had been put on hold and became ever more distant. He graduated from high school and college, and then began his studies in architecture at McGill University. This is where his dream to ski the South Pole was nearly extinguished for good.

"I always wanted to be an architect," says Kevin. "Even before I took one of those assessments in high school that indicated I should be an architect, I knew I wanted to be one. It's another dream that had always been there for me for as long as I can remember."

Like most aspiring students, he had no idea what his chosen path of study was really like until he walked through the doors of the university. He would immediately discover a profession with a culture of obsession that demanded a sacrifice of everything for its pursuit. "My second day at university was spent on an all-nighter trying to get a project done that could never be completed in time," he says. "The professors knew this and were intentionally setting a tone for our next five years in the university and for our next 40 years in the profession—if you want be an architect, forget about everything else."

By the end of his first year Kevin was a wreck. "I had given up on everything important to me," he recalls. "I rarely saw my family and friends anymore. I stopped exercising altogether and I was eating like crap. I was doing well enough in school but everything else had gone to hell."

Second year was harder still, and Kevin remained buried in his studies until just two weeks before Christmas. That's when everything changed. "It was Wednesday evening in the design studio, and we were all working on our end-of-semester design projects that were due on Friday," he says. "No one was close to being finished and we all pulled an all-nighter that night. I remember my friends Dave and Julie—they had been sweethearts since first year—staying up, too, and dealing with it better than the rest of us. They had each other, I suppose, and we fed off their energy."

Wednesday night blurred into Thursday as Kevin and his classmates stayed up for a second night to complete their projects. "We presented our work on the Friday and I was completely exhausted and barely awake," Kevin recalls. "At the end of a long day, we were all heading home, and Dave and Julie piped up to say they were heading out. 'We're going dancing,' they said. 'You should join us!' I remember laughing at them. 'You guys are nuts!' I said back. 'I'm going home to sleep. I'll see you guys in the morning!'"

The following morning brought a three-hour freehand drawing class, the last class of the semester. Kevin remembers pushing through the heavy wooden doors of the architecture building and immediately knowing something was wrong. "It was the weirdest thing, but right away I sensed something," he recalls. "I couldn't explain it. As I walked up the winding stone staircase to the third floor, I just had this strange feeling. Then I thought I heard crying." When he reached the third floor, he saw several classmates walking around in a daze and a group huddled together. In the center of the group was Julie. As Kevin approached, she turned to him and their eyes locked. "I'd never seen an expression like that before," he says. "The sorrow in it. Julie's eyes empty, her face gaunt, I could see she was lost."

The night before, she and Dave had gone out dancing as they'd promised. As they were dancing, Dave collapsed and died of a heart attack. He died in her arms. He was only 19 years old.

"I remember that moment like yesterday," Kevin recalls. "I stumbled out of the building and just started to walk. I remember it was really cold. I didn't care. I just walked. After, I don't know how long, I finally I stopped and just sat down in the snow. I bawled my eyes out."

We all experience moments in our lives when everything changes, when everything beyond that point in time will be different. This was that moment for Kevin. "I remember sitting there in the snow, thinking to myself, I couldn't go on like this. I wouldn't go on like this!" he says. "I promised myself at that exact moment that I was going to change my life. I was going to take care of myself better and seek a balance in my life. From that point forward everything was going to be different."

The next three-and-a-half years of school saw Kevin spending more time with friends and family. He returned to cycling. He had been an active road cyclist before he started architecture, but had all but given it up with the workload from school. He began racing again and steadily rose to an elite level on both road and track. His athletic demands required he eat well and sleep better, too. Before he knew it, Kevin was back to leading a more balanced life. He stuck to his promise to himself.

"I really didn't care how well I did in school anymore," he said. "I decided to enjoy the process rather than fixate on it. I expected my grades would drop, but strangely, they improved. By the time I graduated, I was at the top of my class. I won the Royal Architectural Institute of Canada Medal as top graduating student, and I earned a Commonwealth Scholarship to Cambridge University."

Kevin learned that being consumed by architecture and doing nothing else actually hurt his capacity to excel. He discovered that by balancing his life and spending more quality time with the things he was engaged with, not only improved their outcomes but also required him less time. It was an epiphany. "I also realized that life was short," he says. "And I had a dream to ski to the South Pole. I wasn't going to let that go."

How had Kevin kept going? Why hadn't he quit? For all those years, ever since he was a 10-year-old boy, he held onto his dream to ski to the South Pole and he hadn't quit. How did he do it?

What Is Personal Sustainability?

According to the Center for Nature and Leadership, the definition of personal sustainability, which Kevin has been modeling since that fateful winter day in Montreal, is one's ability to maintain an even or positive balance of personal energy and is the critical starting point for people making a difference in the world.[1] It has been core to Kevin's life philosophy and not only has allowed him to keep going as an elite adventurer but also has provided him with the ability to accomplish more in everything he does.

No doubt, Kevin's adventure exploits are incredibly impressive. His expedition résumé is stacked with journeys that would be a singular lifetime accomplishment for anyone. Not only has Kevin broken the world record in 2009 for the fastest unsupported trek to the South Pole, but he has also skied Alaska's 1,100-mile Iditarod trail in winter, set a speed record trekking the length of Siberia's 400-mile frozen Lake Baikal, and retraced the steps of the infamous Sandakan Death March in Borneo for the first time since World War II. In 2013, he and three teammates attempted to row the notorious Northwest Passage solely under human power in a single season for the first time in history. He led his wife and two young daughters on a 45-day kayak expedition down the 1,100-mile-long Mackenzie River to the Arctic Ocean, and in 2018 he led a team of 11 across Canada's frozen Baffin Island in the high Arctic. And believe it or not, the list goes on.

The sheer number of successful expeditions Kevin has accomplished would be amazing enough, but his exploits don't stop there. In addition to being a world-class adventurer, Kevin has founded and runs an award-winning architectural firm and is a sought-after keynote speaker and leadership trainer. He is a writer—he is the coauthor of this book—and he is a happily married father of two daughters. You wouldn't be the first to ask, "How does he do it?" It's a question that's been elicited a lot.

Kevin Vallely and his family on their 1,100-mile Arctic kayak journey down the Mackenzie River, the longest river in Canada
Courtesy of Kevin Vallely

Setting Boundaries

At first glance, it may appear that Kevin sets no boundaries on himself and takes on everything he sets his mind to, but that evaluation would be inaccurate. For as many things that Kevin has embraced and succeeded at, he's stepped away from just as many too. "I pursued bicycle racing with a passion early in my twenties," he says. "I was pretty good at it, but over time, I realized that the effort versus reward wasn't worth it for me and I stepped away from the sport. Until I found my ideal direction in architecture, I moved in and out of the profession a number of times. I tried working in the film industry but realized the work–life balance in that line of work didn't suit me. I worked as an architectural illustrator, but discovered painting other architects' buildings, although lucrative, was not satisfying for me either, so I stopped. I was the editor-at-large for a travel magazine, an apparent dream job on the surface, but again, not for me, and I walked. I could go on. Ultimately, I discovered the things I really enjoyed doing, and I kept doing them the way I wanted to do them. Again, just like I was willing to say 'no' to a career direction if it didn't suit me, I was also willing to say 'no' to opportunities on my chosen path if they weren't ideal either."

As professionals, many of us get in the habit of saying "yes" to everything that comes our way even when we know we shouldn't or don't want to. It may manifest from a fear of disappointing others or fear of missing out. Or that if we say "no," the opportunity will pass and we may not get another chance. But no matter what the reason, deeply considering those things we say "yes" to is important. Is it to please others, or is it the right thing for you? Of course, from time to time, we may find ourselves in a position where we can't say "no" to a task or request, but if this happens too often, it may require a deeper reflection on why you are doing what you do.

Setting boundaries on ourselves is critical in maintaining the energy we need to sustain long-term performance. But all too often, instead of doing this, we jump at everything that comes our way and become solely focused on what has to be done today, this week, this month, or this quarter. This short-term single-mindedness can often lead to exhaustion and burnout, a condition, described by Monique Valcour in her article "Beating Burnout," that "comprises profound physical, cognitive, and emotional fatigue that undermines people's ability to work effectively and feel positive about what they're doing."[2] Being able to set boundaries on the work we do and the amount of time we spend doing it is one of the simplest ways to prevent burnout and sustain long-term performance and can be done by following the old adage, "control what you can." None of us are fully in control of our time and responsibilities but by addressing the things that we can control and by setting reasonable limits on the work we do and the time we spend doing it, we will go a long way to achieving optimal performance.

Ultradian Rhythms

Another method of boundary setting for long-term performance is gauging how you work. Recognizing that we all have physical and emotional limits and that human beings are not meant to work 24 hours a day, 7 days a week is an important realization. Our bodies cycle between periods of high and low productivity during the course of a day as dictated by our ultradian rhythms. If we can learn to work in concert with them, rather than in spite of them, we will greatly enhance our performance. In their book *The Power of Full Engagement*, Jim Loehr and Tony Schwartz point out that "ultradian rhythms help to account for the ebb and flow of our energy throughout the day. Physiological measures such as heart rate, hormonal levels, muscle tension and brain-wave activity all increase during the first part of the cycle—and so does alertness. After an hour or so, these measures start to decline. Somewhere between 90 and 120 minutes, the body begins to crave a period of rest and recovery."[3]

How often have you experienced a day of nonstop, back-to-back phone calls or meetings, skipping lunch or even simple restroom breaks, only to fuel up with coffee to keep you going? Well, most of us have, and we all know it doesn't work very well in the long term. By understanding your ultradian rhythms, you can get more work done when your body and mind are at their best and get the rest you need when you need it to restore.

We work at our best when we act like the proverbial hare rather than the tortoise. Yes, that's right, working constantly all day will get the job done, but it won't get it done the most effectively. If you want to work at your best, work in spurts with breaks in between.

"Every 90 to 120 minutes, your body has a period of significant energy and alertness followed by a period of fatigue. During that burst of energy, you can work *with* your body to get far more done. During the low point of the cycle, you have to work against your body's natural rhythms to accomplish much at all, which is often a losing battle."[4]

The standard workday was not designed for productivity in mind but rather to keep employees in one place for a set period of time. The thought that an 8-to-5 shift with a half hour for lunch meant eight and a half hours of actual productive work is being naïve. We're not machines, and trying to emulate one will lead to burnout. Unfortunately, organizations are typically not effective in helping leaders deal with information flow and scheduling, so it is even more critical to control these aspects of how you work. "If you're not intentional about scheduling your day around your ultradian rhythms, someone else will schedule your day for you."[5]

Recognizing our biological limits and working within them is essential to achieving our best. Driving ourselves consistently without breaks will not produce the results we hope to achieve. Finding balance is critical and is something Kevin demonstrates exceptionally well.

Balancing Your Energies

On a sprawling campus just outside of the Australian capital of Canberra, you will find a multitude of Australia's sporting elite honing their skills to become the best athletes in the world. They are enrolled at the Australian Institute of Sport, an academy that has become a global leader in discovering and developing athletic potential and espouses a slightly different approach than you might imagine. The AIS was born from failure when Australia was humbled at the 1976 Olympics in Montreal, Canada. Normally a powerhouse in sport, the Australian team collected a meager one silver and four bronze medals[6] and the nation was left stunned. With such a small population and its ignoble beginnings as a penal colony, Australia has long used athletic prowess as a way of distinguishing itself. The poor showing was a national embarrassment and the government created the Australian Institute of Sport to make things different. It worked.

In the 1988 Olympics in Seoul, the Australians won 14 medals; in the 1992 Olympics in Barcelona, they won 27 medals; and by year 2000, when the Olympics were held on home turf in Sydney, the Australian team brought home a whopping 58 medals. The results were astounding. How had they done it?

Using a combination of specific training, technology, and analyzing how an athlete performs in both the short term and the long term, the AIS created a powerful mechanism to achieve peak performance. The AIS research revealed that training harder and longer wasn't the magic elixir at all, but rather pointed to taking a more holistic approach as the best way to achieve peak performance. They discovered that maintaining balance and abundance in all areas of the athlete's life was as vital to an athlete's performance as any specific training.

For most high-performance athletes, like business professionals, long-term sustainable performance draws from four areas of energy—mental, relationship, emotional, and physical. Taking a more balanced approach to the training of their athletes, the AIS were able to transform what was once a beleaguered athletic program into one of the best in the world. Similarly, as a business leader, being more intentional about your own performance in each of these energies can yield better results over the long term.

Let's take a closer look at each of these energies and see how they drive sustainable high performance.

Mental Energy

For most hard-working professionals, having strong mental energy is of paramount importance. The pace and rate in which change happens in the modern global economy requires tremendous amounts of focus and intellectual output, and there is little surprise that mental energy is an area most business professionals emphasize at the expense of others. But how many of us truly consider what our brains need for the highest levels of mental performance?

A wide body of research in the last 10 years around deliberate practice and expertise shows a need to take breaks throughout the day to maintain focus and clarity. As we discussed before, our ultradian rhythms dictate that our periods of optimal productivity are 90 to 120 minutes followed by a break. How many of us adhere to this? From the work of sleep researcher Nathan Kleitman,[7] to the findings of Anders Ericsson[8] and Malcom Gladwell,[9] who focus on expertise and performance, it is clear that for us to optimally grow capacity and sustainability, we need to recognize our natural cycles.

An interesting piece of research from David Rock and Daniel Siegel of the NeuroLeadership Institute has pointed to seven daily essential mental activities necessary for optimum mental health. They equate their seven daily essentials for a healthy mind to the dietary nutritional guidelines for a healthy body. According to Rock and Siegel, of the seven daily essential mental activities to optimize brain matter and create well-being, there are three that are really critical for mental performance. These include "*Focus Time*: When we closely focus on tasks in a goal-oriented way, we take on challenges that make deep connections in the brain; *Play Time*: When we allow ourselves to be spontaneous or creative, playfully enjoying novel experiences, we help make new connections in the brain; and *Down Time*: When we are nonfocused, without any specific goal, and let our mind wander or simply relax, we help the brain recharge."[10]

Rock and Siegel don't prescribe a specific amount of time you should designate for each mental activity but rather encourage us to be conscious of all of these times and to make efforts to engage each for at least some time each day. "When we vary the focus of attention with this spectrum of mental activities, we give the brain lots of opportunities to develop in different ways."[11] According to their research, integrating these elements into your behavior each day "strengthens your brain's internal connections and your connections with other people and the world around you."[12]

Relationship Energy

We are social animals and we thrive through our social connections. Research shows that social connections are as much a basic human need as water, food, and shelter.[13] Our relationships are linked directly to our physical health and our subjective well-being.[14] Spending quality time with the people who matter most can have a significant impact on your physical and mental health and is a critical factor in resilience, longevity, and sustainable performance.

In a recent study by the Connected Commons research initiative, researchers interviewed a diverse group of people from a variety of industries and positions, "and found again and again that flourishing in your career depends as much on your relationships, both in and out of work, as it does on your job itself." The social connections you make "play a central role in fostering a sense of purpose and well-being in the workplace."[15] They help your capacity to learn and to share knowledge, they help you avoid burnout and exhaustion, and they inspire creativity and innovation. An organization that recognizes the importance of social connectedness will have more engaged employees who perform better and are more likely to stick around.

Studies also show that people who thrive at work are anchored in at least one or two nonwork communities.[16] This broad approach to networking beyond work buffers the challenges we face on the job and gives us perspective and allows us to "tap into aspects of our identity that don't rise and fall with how well things are going in the office."[17]

Whether it's in or outside of work, the importance of our relationships can't be overstated. Fostering a strong social network is as important to your overall fulfillment as the very work you do.

Emotional Energy

"When people take more control of their emotions, they can improve the quality of their energy, regardless of the external pressures they're facing." These words are from Tony Schwartz and Catherine McCarthy in their article "Manage Your Energy, Not Your Time" in the *Harvard Business Review*. The two consultants are experts in the field of energy management and espouse that "individuals need to recognize the costs of energy-depleting behaviors and then take responsibility for changing them, regardless of the circumstances they're facing."[18]

As the need for emotional intelligence soars in our changing world, there has been significantly more focus paid to how our emotions not only impact our work, but how they can bolster or hamper our performance. Since the global financial crisis of 2008, many organizations have shifted toward enabling people to more effectively deal with their emotions at work. Gone are the days of excusing temper tantrums from star employees. Today, it is about understanding and learning how to regulate emotions during constant stress and recognizing that not everything is an emergency or crisis. Two powerful methods of controlling your emotions and managing your emotional energy can be done through the practice of regulation and mindfulness. Both practices require an individual to pause and distance themselves from negative emotions they are feeling and ultimately transcend to a better place.

First, emotional regulation is the process of identifying the physical manifestations of an emotion on your body when it's happening. You may be in a meeting, for instance, in which a controversial topic comes up and you're on point to present a viewpoint that you know is going to spark debate. Your stomach churns, the room feels warm, and your heart starts to beat faster. You're feeling anxious about speaking and your body is reacting to it with a fight-or-flight response. Emotional regulation involves stopping in that moment, taking a deep breath, and labeling the feeling, whether jotting it down on a piece of paper or saying it to yourself in your head: "I feel anxious." The labeling of the emotion quickly shifts your biological response back into the cognitive response you'd likely prefer at this moment, allowing you a second to compose more rational thoughts versus a highly charged emotional reaction that you may have blurted out. Regulation certainly isn't easy, and in-the-moment redirection of emotions takes practice, but with practice comes habit and with habit comes skill.

Another effective method of improving your emotional regulation is done through the practice of mindfulness.[19] "Research has shown that mindfulness can change the physiology of the body and brain in ways that strengthen, heal and protect." It reduces stress, anxiety, pain, depression, insomnia, and high blood pressure while restoring emotional balance and resilience. In its simplest form, "mindfulness is the psychological process of bringing one's attention to experiences occurring in the present moment" while "tuning out" all other sensory input.[20] It's the act of being intensely aware of your senses and feelings without any judgment.

Practicing mindfulness can involve breathing methods, guided imagery, and other methods to tune into your senses to relax the body and mind and help reduce stress.[21] Concentrating on slow steady breathing is core to the practice and is an important reason why regular mindfulness exercise can assist in emotional regulation. Being acutely aware of changes to your breathing can indicate when an emotion is about to manifest itself and allows you those split seconds to acknowledge and regulate them before they take control.

Both the practices of regulation and mindfulness help you monitor your emotions and manage your emotional energy, allowing you to rationally control your actions instead of having your emotions in the driver's seat.

Physical Energy

Physical energy is all about being at our most robust on a physiological level. It is generated from adequate sleep, good nutrition, and plenty of exercise. It's what the doctor tells you to do, and we intuitively know how important it as. Human beings are flesh and blood, and everything we do starts with the physical. Building physical energy is one of the fastest and most effective ways to have an impact on your overall performance in each of the other energy components.

John Ratey is a Harvard researcher and an expert on understanding the linkage between physical activity and mental health and has found that "exercise influences brain function, planning, scheduling, inhibition, and working memory."[22] In his book *Spark: The Revolutionary New Science of Exercise and the Brain*, he details example after example of how physical exercise boosts nearly all aspects of mental performance throughout our lives and also grows our capacity.[23] We're physical beings and our minds are as much part of our biology network as our muscles.

A recent study published in *The Lancet Psychiatry* indicates that just two hours of any form of exercise per week will have measureable benefits on one's overall mental health. "One of the nice things is the accessibility of this," says study coauthor Adam Chekroud, an assistant professor of psychiatry at Yale University. "It seems like some of the benefits are pretty in reach for most people."[24] The Centers for Disease Control and Prevention's Behavioral Risk Factor Surveillance System survey reached over 1.2 million people between 2011 and 2015, and the findings indicated that respondents who exercised moderate amounts experienced roughly half the number of gloomy days per month than their sedentary counterparts.

Building our physical energy requires us to recuperate adequately as well, and getting an adequate amount of sleep is critical to this. Oftentimes, when we get busy, sleep is what we sacrifice first. We work late, stay up later, and hit it hard again the next morning. The rigorous cycle of hard work and little sleep becomes a sort of badge of honor rather than an effective way to enhance our performance. We need adequate sleep to perform at our best. In his book *8 Steps to High Performance: Focus on What You Change (Ignore the Rest)*, author Mark Effron culls through research on performance and states unequivocally that "six to seven hours is the ideal range."[25] According to Effron, cutting back on sleep or having a bad night's sleep may impact your ability to emotionally regulate and remember things you would normally would.

In their *Deloitte Insights* article "You Snooze, You Win," Jen Fisher, Susan Hogan, and Amy Fields discuss that "from an organizational perspective, a lack of sleep often has a direct impact on workplace performance. People's ability to learn, concentrate, and retain information is greatly impacted by how well-rested they are. Insufficient sleep causes individuals to be more emotionally unstable, or moody, and has been tied to aggression and forgetfulness. Preliminary research also suggests that individuals who lack sufficient sleep are more prone to unethical behavior. These factors can yield negative consequences for organizational teamwork and individual performance."[26]

Our physical energy is our gateway energy, and simply put, if it's not strong, none of our other energies will be at their best. Achieving peak performance depends heavily on maintaining a robust physical energy through adequate sleep, a nutritional diet, and moderate exercise.

Kevin Vallely has proven himself a paragon of the four energies. Over the course of his life, Kevin has demonstrated an innate capacity to maintain a balance and abundance in each of the four energies, and as a result, has achieved success over a wide range of varied pursuits. He promised to himself after the death of his classmate, David, that he would take better care of himself and after over three decades he has kept this promise.

"Back in architectural school, the belief was that the harder you worked, the better you became," he says. "It took a brutal lesson for me to realize this wasn't the case at all." Right after David's passing, Kevin decided to reengage with the things he had sacrificed when he started architectural school. He returned to his love of bicycle racing, and because of the physical demands of that sport, he needed to and began to eat better and sleep more. He reconnected with friends he hadn't seen in years and spent more time at home with family. He was still passionate about the field of architecture and pursued his studies with disciplined energy and focus, but instead of letting his studies take over his life, he now placed them alongside the other things that were important to him as well.

Kevin anticipated his marks would drop with his reprioritization, but much to his surprise, he began to flourish. By the end of his architectural studies he won the RAIC medal as top graduating student and won a Commonwealth Scholarship for post-graduate work at Cambridge University in England. By balancing his physical, mental, relationship, and emotional energies, Kevin discovered his true potential. He has carried this newfound understanding into everything he does and has become a "master of all trades and a jack of none."

Kevin Vallely enduring −40°F conditions in Lake Baikal, Siberia   *Courtesy of Kevin Vallely*

"How do you keep going? Why don't you quit?" That question from the young offender would dog Kevin all the way to the South Pole. He knew he had an answer for the young man, Sammy, but it wasn't until he reached the South Pole did he discover what it was. Kevin and his two teammates arrived at the South Pole after 33 days, 23 hours, and 55 minutes, breaking the world record for the fastest unsupported journey from the edge of the Antarctic continent to the Geographic South Pole by a team, taking nearly 6 days off the previous fastest mark.

"We had a satellite phone with us, and I gave my mom a call right away," says Kevin. "She was so happy and so relieved to hear from me. I could hear the emotion in her voice and it stirred it in me too. She told me how incredibly proud she was of me, how I'd persisted for so long, how I'd overcome so many challenges in reaching my goal. And, she said, the most important thing that I'd done was, through it all, was that I kept believing in myself. You know, when she said that, I felt like I was ten years old again after struggling through that storm in Montreal. I believed in myself then, and I suppose, I've never stopped believing. I knew right then I had an answer for Sammy."

Throughout his life, Kevin has set boundaries for himself. He's recognized when things were worth struggling for and when they weren't. After the death of his friend, he learned that balancing his life was the way he was going to be his best. He challenged the culture that was the architectural profession and went after, and succeeded at, a disparate number of pursuits because he knew how to take care of himself and balance his life. But above it all, he believed in himself and his capacity to succeed.

"Sammy, I've always felt that if you don't believe in yourself, why should anyone else believe in you? At the very least, give yourself that opportunity and believe in yourself. If you do, you'll never quit."

How to Build Your Personal Sustainability

1. **Setting boundaries.** Recognize that saying "yes" to everything will quickly lead to burnout. We are not wells of limitless time and energy, and we need to set boundaries around what is most important to us and then devote full energy to those passions.

2. **Acknowledging your ultradian rhythms.** Working to align your work with the high and low points of your ultradian rhythms will help balance your overall energy and capacity and will drive improved performance.

3. **Fueling your four energies.** Appreciate that you are an interconnected system and that your four energies of mental, relationship, emotional, and physical energy need to be in balance and abundance for both short-term performance and long-term sustainability.

Conclusion

ew activities test us like an adventure does. This uniquely
human undertaking has the capacity to distill a life's worth
of challenges into a brief interval of time and impart learning
that can inform everything we do. Adventurers actively seek out
challenges to test themselves and transcend the trials of everyday
life, but in undertaking those adventures they also unconsciously
better equip themselves to deal with those very everyday trials.
For those adventurers we mentioned at the start of the book,
answering Shackleton's provocative newspaper call in 1913, they
would experience the exact challenges they had so boldly signed
up for: a *hazardous journey with small wages, bitter cold, long
months of complete darkness, and constant danger.* These men of the
Imperial Trans-Antarctic expedition of 1914 to 1917 would be
confronted with conditions so harsh and challenging that historians today suggest that few, if any, of them would have survived
if it was not for the inspired leadership of Sir Ernest Shackleton.
What made Shackleton's style of leadership so effective? What
is it about this man that has stirred people to reverence, calling him "the greatest leader that ever came on God's earth, bar
none?"[1] Shackleton's Endurance Expedition, which it has come
to be called, was a testament of resilience and fortitude in the

face of unsurmountable odds and is one of the greatest survival stories ever told. There is much to be learned from its intrepid leader that we use to inform our leadership today.

It was August 8, 1914, when Shackleton and his team had set sail from Plymouth, England, in hopes of making the first full land crossing of the Antarctic continent. Their intent was to reach Antarctica early in the new year, but unseasonably thick sea ice would hinder their progress and they would become frozen-in miles off the Antarctic coast, never making land. Their ship, *The Endurance*, would remain beset in the sea ice throughout the winter of 1915 and would eventually be crushed and sink, stranding the entire 28-man crew atop the ice. In makeshift camps, the crew would survive the next several months until they were forced to make a dash by lifeboat to desolate Elephant Island as the ice broke up. The remote island sits at the pointy end of Antarctica's archipelago and is exposed to the wild storms of the Southern Ocean. It is utterly isolated and completely unfit for long-term survival. There was no rescue coming, and everyone knew it.

Despite it all, Ernest Shackleton remained the unwavering leader, completely in charge, inspiring optimism and emanating confidence in their hope for survival. Shackleton intuitively understood that during trying times like this, hierarchies and factions would arise and discontent would manifest. He set about establishing a strict routine and order among his men and kept the malcontents close to him to subdue their disquiet. He knew the expedition team had only each other to survive, and he had to do everything to maintain this critical human bond and a feeling of unity.

Because of the remoteness of Elephant Island, the teams' only chance of escape was to make a perilous 800-mile journey across the Southern Ocean to South Georgia Island where a manned whaling station at Stromness could help rally a rescue. "Old Cautious," as Shackleton was nicknamed, was typically very conservative in his decision-making, but like every great leader, he knew when to make bold decisions and act. This was that time. Shackleton assembled five of his best men and set off across one of the most ferocious bodies of water on the planet in a tiny 22.5-foot rowboat called the *James Caird*, risking everything for the salvation of his team. Incredibly, they would successfully make the journey and would go down in the annals of history as completing one of the boldest ocean journeys ever attempted. But it wasn't over yet.

When they reached the south shore of South Georgia, the *James Caird* was in tatters and two of the crew had taken ill. The team of five landed at King Haakon Bay, rested, and faced another vexing problem. The whaling station where they were navigating to at Stromness was on the northeast side of the island, but they were on the western side. Navigating the failing *James Caird* with two ailing crew members was not feasible for the team, so Shackleton, with two healthy men, decided to cross the island on foot. South Georgia is a mountainous and heavily glaciated island, and again, Shackleton defied all the odds and made it across South Georgia in a 36-hour nonstop push. To put this one small section of this inconceivable ordeal into perspective, in April 2000, three of the world's most accomplished climbers, Stephen Venables, Reinhold Messner, and Conrad Anker, retraced Shackleton's route across South Georgia and struggled with the difficulty of the challenge presented. For Shackleton and his two crew members, Frank Worsley and Tom Crean, this represented just one small and unbelievably difficult chapter in an epic journey of truly heroic proportion. And even at this, Sir Ernest Shackleton's journey as a leader was far from over. Eight hundred miles away, on a distant rocky outcrop in the middle of the Southern Ocean waited 22 men, desperately needing rescue.

Over the course of the next three months, Shackleton would be stymied in his efforts to reach his men. His first attempt was just a few days after retrieving his ailing team from the western shore of South Georgia Island. He secured the use of a large whaler called *The Southern Sky* that had been laid up on South Georgia, but after journeying to Elephant Island he met with impenetrable pack ice some 70 miles from shore. He retreated to the Falkland Islands and a month later gave it another shot using a tough Uruguayan trawler, but again was thwarted by the pack ice. Searching for another ship, Shackleton traveled to Punta Arenas, Chile, and met a British expat who loaned him the use of his schooner, the *Emma*. But again Shackleton would encounter impenetrable pack ice and would be forced to return to Punta Arenas. By mid-August, he was desperate and time was running out. In a last-ditch effort, he convinced the Chilean government to lend him a small steam tug called *Yelcho* to make one more attempt. On August 30, 1916, over four months after he left his 22 crewmen, Sir Ernest Shackleton returned to Elephant Island and rescued his men. The expedition is considered one of the greatest feats of endurance in the history of exploration. Not a single life was lost on the journey. Through it all, Shackleton proved himself a masterful leader who through an unfaltering display of coolness under pressure, crisis management, and resilience guided his crew through an ordeal so challenging that there really is no equal.

As the years have passed, countless books and articles have been written about Shackleton's heroic leadership skills, all pointing to an unflappable champion displaying exemplary skills with no weakness. So (Kevin speaking here) you could imagine my surprise when I discovered that Shackleton was very human after all. It was November 2008 and I was walking the streets of Punta Arenas, Chile, just prior to traveling to Antarctica for my own expedition to the South Pole. I came across a plaque at the entrance to the Chalet Milward in the center of town. It read: "In 1916, Claude Milward lodged the explorer Ernest Shackleton, who due to a nervous breakdown during his organization of a rescue of his companions on Elephant Island, fired several shots which are still encrusted in the walls of the main drawing room." I was stunned.

It would appear that the unshakable Shackleton was, in fact, human after all. It was an astonishing discovery simply because it had been removed from the narrative of the man. Shackleton, the hero, having a nervous breakdown doesn't equate with the persona being plied, but maybe it's time we look a little deeper into that character. Ernest Shackleton did what few others could ever do and proved himself a leader beyond reproach. The fact that he suffered a nervous breakdown simply speaks to his humanity and suggests a more astonishing personality than the one we first thought. Even after enduring his own personal setback, Shackleton was still able to rebound, acquire another ship, and rescue his men. He built himself up again to be the best that he could be and succeeded. The fact that he, too, is fallible, just like the rest of us, is reassuring, but the fact that he is able to rebound and succeed, is truly inspiring. What it suggests is that Shackleton's equally impressive characteristics—all very human characteristics, too—are equally accessible to us all. And this is the thesis of *Wild Success*.

Just like Sir Ernest Shackleton, the adventurers we have profiled in this book are all remarkable individuals who are paragons of performance, but they are human, too. The amazing traits they display are skills they have finely honed, skills that can be practiced, learned, and mastered. We can all drive ourselves to higher performance, but just like these adventurers, we must want to, too.

In this book you have met big-wave surfer Mark Mathews, a master of his craft, surfing waves the size of buildings. Mark has shown us that the ability to cognitively reappraise is an exceptionally valuable skill, but as simple and straightforward as it appears, requires dedication and practice to become routine. Much like the salesperson who reframes a "no" into an opportunity to continue to refine his or her pitch, it requires a dedicated practice and habit to deal with our emotions. For those individuals who can make it a habit, like Mark, the outcomes are immediate, profound, and life changing.

We have followed the journey of Paul Gleeson and Tori Holmes and discovered how an offhand question from a friend became an inextinguishable angst for both Paul and Tori who then because of their unrelenting grit built their passion into action and successfully rowed 4,700 kilometers across the Atlantic Ocean. They teach us that crafting our own story and controlling what we can allows us to shift from novices to believers.

Adventurer Matt McFadyen demonstrated to us that "the view you adopt for yourself profoundly affects the way you lead your life."[2] These words from Dr. Carol Dweck speak to how Matt McFadyen has accomplished all he has, extricating himself from humble beginnings in Australia to become an internationally recognized explorer and leadership professional. Matt believed in himself and his abilities, and because of it, chartered his own course to success. We will all face "out of our element" challenges in which we can approach with openness to feedback and hard work that will affect how we come out the other side.

We were introduced to the irrepressible spirit of Roz Savage, who after undertaking a self-reflection exercise by writing her own obituary, realized she needed to radically change her life to find her own true purpose. She changed her life, became an ocean rower, and began to explore what she was meant to do. She now holds four Guinness World Records for ocean rowing and uses her notoriety as one of the world's most accomplished adventurers to proclaim her environmental message. Roz's sense of purpose has matured through her rowing career, with one idea being supported by the next, and she now has reached a point in her life where she confidently feels she can truly be in the service of others. She has found her purpose. Like Roz, you can look inside to find your own spark and reap the benefits not only with your work, but with your health and longevity, too.

In this book, we learned how the evolution of Rex Pemberton from an adventure-hungry high school student to groundbreaking extreme athlete speaks to the power of innovation. In profiling Rex's career, we discovered that you need to be a dreamer to be innovative and that hard struggle is a necessary part of that game. It hasn't come easy for Rex, or for any of the adventurers profiled in *Wild Success*, but by pushing the boundaries of what's considered possible, he, like the others, has built a remarkable capacity for insight and creativity. Recognizing both your capacity for dreaming big and realizing the accompanying struggle to make those dreams a reality is a tactical way of approaching innovation that can lead you more effectively to new ideas.

You witnessed how in just a split-second Lisa Blair went from being on track to break the world record for the fastest solo, nonstop sailing circumnavigation of Antarctica to fighting for her life. It was a brutal test for the young Australian who, after narrowly escaping catastrophe, limped into Cape Town, South Africa, and was left with a difficult choice to make: call it quits or head back into the cauldron that nearly took her life. Lisa would choose to continue her journey, and not because she was reckless, but rather because she was resilient and knew exactly what she could do. Her lessons of preparing for the worst and sustaining those relationships that can buoy you in your toughest times help us with our own setbacks and trials.

And finally, we met Kevin Vallely, the coauthor of *Wild Success*, who throughout his life has set boundaries for himself that have been critical to his success. As a young man he challenged the culture that was the architectural profession and discovered the power of personal sustainability. He realized that if he took care of himself and balanced his life, he could thrive at anything he pursued. His fundamental belief in himself has underpinned his capacity to succeed and inspires those around him to fuel their own success differently by living with intention and making deliberate choices.

Our hope is that you have come away engaged and inspired by the stories we've shared with you from both the adventure and business worlds, and that the performance tips and tactics we have distilled from these experiences will let you grow and thrive as a leader. The allure of adventure is to experience the unknown and to draw from it a different way of seeing the world. By reading *Wild Success* you've had the opportunity to look through the lens of the extreme adventurer and see and experience the world like few others do. We hope it has emboldened you to chart your own new course and achieve your own *Wild Success*. Thank you for joining us on this journey!

> *I went to the woods because I wished to live deliberately, to front only the essential facts of life, and see if I could not learn what it had to teach, and not, when I came to die, discover that I had not lived.*
> **—HENRY DAVID THOREAU**

Notes

For those of you who are notes readers in books, welcome! You are an intrepid reader, and we thank you for going deeper into this book and the references and resources we've used to shape the stories and tips provided within. One of our goals in writing this book was to use more current research that is well-proven. Our focus was on using meta-studies (studies of multiple studies) with high sample sizes and broad application. There are a lot of writers these days using a one-off study with a N=9 and we wanted more for you in *Wild Success*. As you know, research and current thinking changes quickly, and we wrote based on what we know. Any one of these studies could be debunked (and, in fact, one of our readers pointed something out to us that mandated additional thought and writing), but this represents our best effort to provide where science and business is currently at today.

INTRODUCTION

1. Van Wulfen, Gijs, *10 Innovation Lessons from Great Explorers*, LinkedIn.com, Oct. 1, 2012, https://www.linkedin.com/pulse/2012 1002125503-206580-innovation-lessons-from-great-explorers/. Rumor has it that this was an advertisement posted by Sir Ernest Shackleton in the London newspaper the *Times*, but historians have been unable to prove it. Whether it really happened is now up for debate, but there's little question that this call to action was what volunteers knew they were getting themselves into when they joined him on his Imperial Trans-Antarctic Expedition.

CHAPTER 1

1. Butler, C., "Mark Mathews Opens Up About the Physical and Emotional Recovery of a Career-Threatening Wipeout," *The Inertia*, April 30, 2018, https://www.theinertia.com/surf/mark-mathews-opens-up-about-the-physical-and-emotional-recovery-of-a-career-threatening-wipeout/.

2. Mathews, M., "Face Your Biggest Fears and Bounce Back," interview by Lewis Howes, LewisHowes.com, podcast, July 25, 2017, https://lewishowes.com/podcast/h-mark-mathews/.

3. Haro, A., "Mark Mathews on the Wipeout That Might Have Ended His Career," *The Inertia*, February 7, 2017, https://www.theinertia.com/surf/mark-mathews-on-the-wipeout-that-might-havfe-ended-his-career/.

4. Smith, J., "Mark Mathews: 'I Was One Hour from Losing My Leg,'" *Stab Magazine*, 2017, https://stabmag.com/news/mark-mathews-i-was-one-hour-from-losing-my-leg/. This particular article has some gruesome pictures of Mark's leg from the operating and recovery room, so it's definitely not for the faint of heart. In fact, if you're squeamish at all, don't even click on this one—the above-the-fold photo is really intense. Don't say we didn't warn you.

5. Mathews, M., "Face Your Biggest Fears and Bounce Back," interview by Lewis Howes, LewisHowes.com, podcast, July 25, 2017, https://lewishowes.com/podcast/h-mark-mathews/.

6. Butler, C., "Mark Mathews Opens Up About the Physical and Emotional Recovery of a Career-Threatening Wipeout," *The Inertia*, April 30, 2018, https://www.theinertia.com/surf/mark-mathews-opens-up-about-the-physical-and-emotional-recovery-of-a-career-threatening-wipeout/.

7. Hutchens, G., "Big Wave Surfer Mark Mathews, His Horrific Injuries and the Battle to Control His Own Fear," *The Guardian*, Jan. 2, 2018, https://www.theguardian.com/sport/2018/jan/03/big-wave-surfer-mark-mathews-his-horrific-injuries-and-the-battle-to-control-his-own-fear.

8. Ibid.

9. Ibid.

10. Ibid.

11. Denson, T. F., Creswell, J. D., Terides, M. D., and Blundell, K., "Cognitive Reappraisal Increases Neuroendocrine Reactivity to Acute Social Stress and Physical Pain," *Psychoneuroendocrinology* 49, (2014): 69–78.

12. Ibid.
13. Troy, A., Wilhelm, F., Shallcross, A., and Mauss, I., "Seeing the Silver Lining: Cognitive Reappraisal Ability Moderates the Relationship Between Stress and Depressive Symptoms." *Emotion* 10, no. 6, (2010): 783–795.
14. Bastiaansen, J., Bennik, E., Marsman, J. B., Ormel, J., Aleman, A., and Oldehinkel, A., "Prefrontal Cortex Activation During a Cognitive Reappraisal Task Is Associated with Real-Life Negative Affect Reactivity," *PLOS One* (2019), https://doi.org/10.1371/journal.pone.0202888.
15. Buhle, J., Silvers, J., Wagner, T., Lopez, R. Onyemekwu, C., Kober, H, Weber, J., and Ochsner, K., "Cognitive Reappraisal of Emotion: A Meta-Analysis of Human Neuroimaging Studies," *Cerebral Cortex* 23, no. 11 (2014): 2981–2990.
16. Yan, C., Lin, N., Cui, L., and Zhang, Q., "Is Reappraisal Always Effective in Modifying Emotional Reactions in Females? The Role of Regulatory Timing and Goals," *Brain and Behavior* (2018), https://doi.org/10.1002/brb3.911.
17. Buhle, J., Silvers, J., Wagner, T., Lopez, R. Onyemekwu, C., Kober, H, Weber, J., and Ochsner, K., "Cognitive Reappraisal of Emotion: A Meta-Analysis of Human Neuroimaging Studies," *Cerebral Cortex* 24, no. 11 (Nov. 1, 2014): 2981–2990, https://doi.org/10.1093/cercor/bht154.
18. Parker-Pope, T., "Writing Your Way to Happiness," *New York Times*, January 19. 2015, https://well.blogs.nytimes.com/2015/01/19/writing-your-way-to-happiness.

CHAPTER 2

1. Stoltz, P., "Leadership Grit," *Leader to Leader*, Sep. 1, 2015.
2. Ibid.
3. Sudbrink, Laurie, "Leveraging Grit for Leadership Success," *Leader to Leader*, Jan. 1, 2016.
4. Holmes, T., Gleeson, P., and Gorman, L., *Crossing the Swell: An Atlantic Journey by Rowboat* (Surrey, BC, Canada: Rocky Mountain Books, 2009).
5. Duckworth, A., *Grit: The Power of Passion and Perseverance* (New York: Scribner, 2016).
6. Gilchrist, J., Fong, A., Herbison, J., and Sabiston, C., "Feelings of Pride Are Associated with Grit in Student-Athletes and Recreational Runners," *Psychology of Sport & Exercise*, Feb. 25, 2017.

7. Duckworth, A., *Grit: The Power of Passion and Perseverance* (New York: Scribner, 2016).
8. Holmes, T., Gleeson, P., and Gorman, L., *Crossing the Swell: An Atlantic Journey by Rowboat* (Surrey, BC, Canada: Rocky Mountain Books, 2009).
9. Ibid.

CHAPTER 3

1. Dweck, C., *Mindset: The New Psychology of Success* (New York: Random House LLC, 2006).
2. Cardero, R., and Derler, A., "4 Steps for Embracing the Discomfort of Developing a Growth Mindset. Your Brain at Work," *Neuroleadership Insitute* (November 29, 2018).
3. Johnston, I., "Creating a Growth Mindset," *Strategic HR Review* 16, no. 4 (August 14, 2017).
4. Dweck, C., "Mindsets and Human Nature," *American Psychologist* 67, no. 8 (November 1, 2012).
5. Ibarra, H., and Rattan, A., "Microsoft: Instilling a Growth Mindset," *London Business School Review* 29, no. 3 (October 1, 2018).
6. Nadella, S., Shaw, G., and Nichols, J., *Hit Refresh: The Quest to Rediscover Microsoft's Soul and Imagine a Better Future for Everyone* (New York: Harper Business, 2017), 113.

CHAPTER 4

1. Savage, R., *Rowing the Atlantic: Lessons Learned on the Open Ocean* (New York: Simon and Schuster, 2010).
2. Duckworth, A., *Grit: The Power of Passion and Perseverance* (New York: Scribner, 2016), 162.
3. Colan, L., "How to Become a Purpose-Driven Leader," Inc.com, https://www.inc.com/lee-colan/how-to-become-a-purpose-driven -leader.html.
4. *Purpose at Work 2016 Global Report*, LinkedIn study, accessed May 2, 2019, https://business.linkedin.com/content/dam/me/business/en-us /talent-solutions/resources/pdfs/purpose-at-work-global-report.pdf.
5. Hotten, R., "Volkswagen: The Scandal Explained," *BBC News*, Dec. 10, 2015, https://www.bbc.com/news/business-34324772.
6. Cone, C., "What Does a Purpose-Driven Company Look Like?" *Salesforce* (blog), July 2019, https://www.salesforce.org/what-does-a-purpose -driven-company-look-like/.

7. Pontefract, D., "Salesforce CEO Marc Benioff Says the Business of Business Is Improving the State of the World," *Forbes*, Jan. 7, 2017, https://www.forbes.com/sites/danpontefract/2017/01/07/salesforce-ceo -marc-benioff-says-the-business-of-business-is-improving-the-state-of -the-world/#5e6e700f7eb0.

8. Brewster, D., Hurst, A., and Schulyer, S., "Making Work More Meaningful: Building a Fulfilling Employee Experience." *Pricewa-terhouseCoopers*, 2016. https://www.pwc.com/us/en/library/workforce -of-the-future/fulfillment-at-work.html

9. Kaplin, A., and Anzaldi, L., "New Movement in Neuroscience: A Purpose-Driven Life," *Cerebrum: The Dana Forum on Brain Science* (June 1, 2015).

10. Marques, J., "Oh What Happiness! Finding Joy and Purpose Through Work," *Development and Learning in Organizations* 31, no. 3 (May 2, 2017).

11. *Purpose at Work 2016 Global Report*, LinkedIn study, accessed May 9, 2019, https://business.linkedin.com/content/dam/me/business/en-us /talent-solutions/resources/pdfs/purpose-at-work-global-report.pdf.

12. Craig, N., and Snook, S., "From Purpose to Impact," *Harvard Business Review* (May 2014).

13. Ibid.

14. We conducted a video interview with Roz Savage to gather her first-person account of how she went about finding her purpose to sup-plement the story she tells in her own book (referenced above).

15. "Job Crafting—Amy Wrzesniewski on Creating Meaning in Your Own Work," YouTube video, posted by re:Work with Google, Nov. 10, 2014, https://www.youtube.com/watch?v=C_igfnctYjA.

16. Ibid.

17. Duckworth, A., *Grit: The Power of Passion and Perseverance* (New York: Scribner, 2016), 145.

18. Ibid., 153.

19. Roz Savage, personal interview, Feb. 22, 2019.

20. Ibid.

CHAPTER 5

1. "Innovation," *Wikipedia*, last modified Nov. 22, 2019, https://en .wikipedia.org/wiki/Innovation.

2. Merriam-Webster OnLine, s.v. "innovation," https://www.merriam -webster.com/dictionary/innovation.

3. Blaszczak-Box, A.,"Daydreaming Again? 5 Facts About the Wandering Mind," Livescience, September 15, 2016, https://www.livescience.com/56096-surprising-facts-about-daydreaming.html.

4. Dell'Amore, C., "Five Surprising Facts About Daydreaming," *National Geographic*, July 16, 2003, https://www.nationalgeographic.com/news/2013/7/130716-daydreaming-science-health-brain/.

5. Sio, U., and Omerod, T., "Does Incubation Enhance Problem Solving? A Meta-Analytic Review," *Psychological Bulletin* 135, no. 1 (2009), 94-120.

6. Yang, H., Chattopadhyay, A., Zhang, K., and Dahl, D., "Unconscious Creativity: When Can Unconscious Thought Outperform Conscious Thought," *Journal of Consumer Psychology* 22, no. 4 (2012), 573-581.

7. Thompson, D., "Google X and the Science of Radical Activity," *The Atlantic*, November 2017, https://www.theatlantic.com/magazine/archive/2017/11/x-google-moonshot-factory/540648/.

8. Google X website, accessed Sept. 9, 2019, https://x.company/

9. Satell, G., "Everybody Should Be Pursuing a Grand Challenge—Here's Why," *Digital Tonto* (Jan. 14, 2018), https://www.digitaltonto.com/2018/everybody-should-be-pursuing-a-grand-challenge-heres-why/.

10. Sutton, R., "Learning from Success and Failure," *Harvard Business Review* (June 4, 2007).

11. Ansburg, P., and Dominowski, R., "Promoting Insightful Problem Solving," *The Journal of Creative Behavior* 34, (2000), 30-60.

12. Kounious, J., and Beeman, M., *The Eureka Factor: Aha Moments, Creative Insight, and the Brain*, (New York: Random House, 2015).

13. Lutfiak, A., Cagri, B., Gurhan, G., Gunduz, U., and Kemal, K., "Organizational Support for Intrapreneurship and Its Interaction with Human Capital to Enhance Innovative Performance," *Management Decision* 48 (2010), 732-755.

14. Rock, D., "Three Ways to Think Deeply at Work," *Harvard Business Review* (September 28, 2012).

15. Kounious, J., and Beeman, M., *The Eureka Factor: Aha Moments, Creative Insight, and the Brain* (New York: Random House, 2015).

16. "Wiping Out Polio: How the US Snuffed Out a Killer," *National Public Radio*, October 15, 2012, https://www.npr.org/sections/health-shots/2012/10/16/162670836/wiping-out-polio-how-the-u-s-snuffed-out-a-killer.

17. Kounious, J., and Beeman, M., *The Eureka Factor: Aha Moments, Creative Insight, and the Brain* (New York: Random House, 2015).
18. Ibid.
19. Jafri, M., Dem, C., and Choden, S., "Emotional Intelligence and Employee Creativity: Moderating Role of Proactive Personality and Organizational Climate," *Business Perspectives and Research* 4, (Jan. 1, 2016).
20. Choi, J., Anderson, T., and Veillette, A., "Contextual Inhibitors of Employee Creativity in Organizations," *Group & Organization Management* 34, no. 3 (2009).
21. Subramaninam, K., Kounious, J., Parrish, T., and Jung-Beeman, M., "A Brain Mechanism for Facilitation of Insight by Positive Affect," *Journal of Cognitive Neuroscience* 21, no. 3 (2009), 415–432.
22. Amabile, T., Barsade, S., Mueller, J., and Staw, B., "Affect and Creativity at Work," *Administrative Science Quarterly* 50 (2005), 367–403.
23. George, J., and Zhou, J. "Understanding When Bad Moods Foster Creativity and Good Ones Don't: The Role of Context and Clarity of Feelings," *Journal of Applied Psychology* 87, no. 4 (August 1, 2002).

CHAPTER 6

1. Konnikova, M., "How People Learn to Become Resilient," *The New Yorker*, February 11, 2016.
2. Werner, E., *Through the Eyes of Innocents: Children Witness World War II* (Boulder, CO: Westview Press, 2000).
3. Ibid.
4. Konnikova, M., "How People Learn to Become Resilient," *The New Yorker* (February 11, 2016).
5. Schoenfeld, T., and Gould, E., "Stress, Stress Hormones, and Adult Neurogenesis," *Experimental Neurology* 233, no. 1 (January 2012).
6. McEwen, B., "Central Effects of Stress Hormones in Health and Disease: Understanding the Protective and Damaging Effects of Stress and Stress Mediators," *European Journal of Pharmacology* 583, nos. 2–3 (April 7, 2008).
7. Sandberg, S., and Grant, A., *Option B: Facing Adversity, Building Resilience, and Finding Joy* (New York: Random House, 2017).
8. Guimarães, R., "Resilience," *Journal of Nutrition, Health and Aging* 22, no. 10 (2018), 1146–47.

9. Kuntz, J., Malinen, S., and Naswall, K., "Employee Resilience: Directions for Resilience Development," *Consulting Psychology Journal: Practice and Research* 69, no. 3: 20 (Sep. 1, 2017).

10. Seligman, M., "Building Resilience," *Harvard Business Review* (April 2011).

11. Goleman, D., "Resilience for the Rest of Us," *Harvard Business Review* (March 2016).

12. Achor, S., and Gielan, M., "Resilience Is About How You Recharge, Not How You Endure," *Harvard Business Review* (June 2016).

13. Levinson, E., and Stapleton, A., "Two Killed in Shooting at Jacksonville Video Game Tournament," *CNN*, August 27, 2018, https://edition.cnn.com/2018/08/26/us/jacksonville-madden-shooting/.

CHAPTER 7

1. *Live Your Legacy Toolkit*, Center for Nature and Leadership, website, accesed Sept. 3, 2019, http://natureleadership.org.

2. Valcour, M., "Beating Burnout," *Harvard Business Review* (June 20, 2016).

3. Loehr, J., and Schwartz, T., *The Power of Full Engagement* (New York: Simon and Schuster, 2005).

4. Thanh Pham, "Tapping into Your Ultradian Rhythms for Max Productivity," *Asian Efficiency* (Sep. 2017).

5. Ibid.

6. McClusky, M., "One One-Hundredth of a Second Faster: Building Better Olympic Athletes," *Wired Magazine* (June 2012), https://www.wired.com/2012/06/ff_superhumans/.

7. Kleitman, N., "Sleep," *Physiological Reviews* 9 (1929), 624.

8. Ericsson, K., "Deliberate Practice and Acquisition of Expert Performance: A General Overview," *Academic Emergency Medicine* 15, no. 11 (2009).

9. Gladwell, M., *Outliers: The Story of Success* (New York: Little, Brown, 2008).

10. Rock, D., Siegel, D., Polemans, S., and Payne, J., "The Healthy Mind Platter," *The NeuroLeadership Journal*, no. 4 (2012).

11. Ibid.

12. Ibid.

13. Ibid.

14. Huppert, F. A., Baylis, B., Keverne, J., Helliwell, R., and Putnam, D., "The Social Context of Well-Being," *Philosophical Transactions of the Royal Society Biological Sciences* (2004).
15. Cross, R., "To Be Happier at Work, Invest More in Your Relationships," *Harvard Business Review* (July 30, 2019).
16. Cross, R., and Grau, R., "The Invisible Network Strategies of Successful People: Counterintuitive Ways to Innovate, Execute, and Thrive at Work," *Connected Commons* (2018).
17. Cross, R., "To Be Happier at Work, Invest More in Your Relationships," *Harvard Business Review* (July 30, 2019).
18. Schwartz, T., and McCarthy, C., "Manage Your Energy, Not Your Time," *Harvard Business Review* (October 2007).
19. Hill, C. and Updegraff, J., "Mindfulness and Its Relationship to Emotional Regulation." *Emotion* 12, no 1, (2012), 81–90.
20. "Mindfulness," *Wikipedia*, last modified 20 November 2019, https://en.wikipedia.org/wiki/Mindfulness.
21. Mayo Clinic Mindfulness Exercises, https://www.mayoclinic.org/healthy-lifestyle/consumer-health/in-depth/mindfulness-exercises/art-20046356.
22. Ratey, J., and Loehr, J., "The Positive Impact of Physical Activity on Cognition During Adulthood: A Review of Underlying Mechanisms, Evidence and Recommendations," *Reviews in the Neurosciences* 22, no. 2 (2011).
23. Ratey, J., *Spark: The Revolutionary New Science of Exercise and the Brain* (New York: Little, Brown, 2008).
24. Ducharme, J., "Exercise Is Good for Your Mental Health—but Only to a Point," *Time Magazine* (August 2018).
25. Effron, M., *8 Steps to High Performance: Focus on What You Can Change (Ignore the Rest)* (Brighton, MA: Harvard Business Review Press, 2018).
26. Fisher, J., Hogan, S., and Fields, A., "You Snooze, You Win: Why Organizations Should Prioritize Having a Well-Rested Workforce," *Deloitte Insights* (February 4, 2019).

CONCLUSION

1. Morrell, M., and Capparell, S., *Shackleton's Way: Leadership Lessons from the Great Antarctic Explorer* (London: 2002).
2. Dweck, C., *Mindset: The New Psychology of Success* (New York: Random House, 2006).

Additional Resources

CHAPTER 2

We used some additional resources for our thinking in this chapter, including Paul's psychology thesis on his own study of grit at Dublin Business School.

Gleeson, P., "The Role of Emotional Well-Being and Internal Locus of Control on Grit," Higher Diploma in Arts in Psychology at Dublin Business School, Dublin Ireland, 2018.

Also, these resources, although not explicitly cited, were interesting in considering other ways to build grit:

Raphiphatthana, B., Jose, P., and Chobthamkit, P., "The Association Between Mindfulness and Grit: An East vs. West Cross-Cultural Comparison," *Mindfulness* 10, no. 1 (May 2018).

Park, S., Kwak, K., and Kim, Y., "Psychological Variables Related to Grit Among Adolescents in South Korea: A longitudinal Study from Age 4–14," *Current Psychology* (August 7, 2018).

Schmidt, F., Nagy, G., Fleckenstein, J., Moller, J., and Retelsdorf, J., "Same Same but Different, Relations Between Facets of Conscientiousness and Grit," *European Journal of Personality* 32 (2018), 705–720.

Acknowledgments

First, we want to personally thank the adventurers profiled in this book who have each shared their lives with us. To Mark Mathews, Paul Gleeson, Tori Holmes, Matt McFadyen, Lisa Blair, Rex Pemberton, Roz Savage, and Shane Toohey, we want to say thank you for your openness and your willingness to share your life experiences with us.

Thank you to the team at McGraw Hill and to our editor, Donya Dickerson. Without meeting Donya and her encouragement to write our proposal and being intrigued with our idea, we would have never made the leap to make this book happen. Thank you as well to Nora Hennick, Amanda Muller, and Amy Li, who have helped guide our way.

Thank you to our AIP Group colleagues in their flexibility when the book needed to take priority. We are endlessly grateful to work with a tremendously talented set of people. A special thanks to Tabitha Stoodley, who lent her creativity to our graphics and cover.

We would also like to thank our amazing clients for sharing their stories and their enthusiasm and encouragement to bring *Wild Success* to life. Thank you to those of you who shared personal stories when we asked for them. Your courage and vulnerability will prompt others in their growth. Even if your story didn't make it in the book, it shaped our thinking and we are so appreciative. Our clients have shaped our perspective and set examples of how we can all learn and grow.

Personal acknowledgments from Amy:

I deeply grateful for my coauthor, Kevin, first and foremost, for being an inspiration on squeezing the most out of life in all he chooses to do. I am grateful he chose to spend this time with me in creating something for which we are both exceptionally proud. His creativity, thoughtfulness, earnestness, and work ethic are all things I admire deeply about him and I know readers will as well.

I am also so grateful for my family and friends who have supported and encouraged this journey as well as all of my adventures along the way. Specifically, I want to thank a group of friends who have been incredibly supportive and helping me face balancing the challenges of career, writing, and adventure. Thank you to Ady Becerra, Sara Noorzay, Tina Randhawa, Stephanie Salisian, and Lisa Schilling. Additional thanks to Morgan Wiley, Amy Cronk, Jen Duran, Karen Lai, Suzanne Leff, and Misty Dodero, who have all been helpful to me during this process.

Last, thank you to Bob Posey. His support, encouragement, and caring have made both this book better and my life better.

Personal acknowledgments from Kevin:

I want to thank my coauthor, Amy Posey, without whom this book would not have happened. Amy brought to the writing profound insights that not only captivated me throughout but inspired me to be the best that I can be. We made a great team producing *Wild Success*, and the fun it was to write only speaks to this connection we shared as well.

And I want to thank my wife, Nicky Hastings, who is always my bastion of support and my partner through it all, and, of course, my two daughters, Caitlin and Arianna, who are always eager to be part of whatever journey we set them on.

This work is really about the greatest adventure of all, life, and what we can make of it in whatever adventures we choose. We wish wild success for all of you.

Index

Achor, Shawn, 148
Advice, seeking, 60–61
AIP Group, viii, xiv, xvi–xviii, 71
AIS (Australian Institute of Sport),
    172–173
Allostatic load, 148–149
Allostatic overload, 142
Alpkan, Lutfihak, 118
Alzheimer's disease, 89–90
Amygdala, 16, 19
Anker, Conrad, 187
Ansburg, Pamela, 117
Antarctica, xiv–xv
AppDynamics, 118–119, 125
Architecture, 120–122
Armstrong, Lance, 41
The Art of Happiness (Dalai Lama), 23
Atlantic Ocean, 96
Atlantic Rowing Race, 96
Australian Institute of Sport (AIS),
    172–173

Baffin Island, x
Balancing of energies, 192
    importance and benefits of,
        166–167
    importance of, 49–50
    for personal sustainability, 172–173,
        180–183

Banga, Ajay, 86–87
BASE jumping, 114–115
Basilica di San Francesco d'Assisi,
    121
"Beating Burnout" (Valcour), 170
Beck, Aaron T., 39
Behavior Risk Factor Surveillance
    System survey, 179
Beliefs, about growth mindset, 63–67
Benioff, Marc, 88
BetterUp, 11–12
Bicycling, 41–42
Blair, Lisa, xiii, 129–137, 139–150,
    152–155, 191–192
Blockbuster, 114
Blood pressure, 144
"Blue-sky thinking," 120
Boundaries, setting, 169–170, 183
Boyle, Patricia, 89–90
Brain, effect of cognitive reappraisal
    on, 16–19
"A Brain Mechanism for Facilitation
    of Insight by Positive Affect," 124
Breaks, and mental energy, 174
"Building Resilience" (Seligman), 148
Buoyancy, 13
Burnout, 170
Business Roundtable Statement of
    Purpose, 88

Callahan, Frankie, 118–119, 125
Calling, 99–100
Cancer, facing, 74–76
Cardero, Rachel, 60
Career:
  job, purpose, and, 85
  lack of following traditional, 90
  passion in, 42–46
Center for Nature and Leadership,
  167
Change(s):
  as opportunity, 112–113
  in professional life, 34–35
Change fatigue, 32
Chekroud, Adam, 179
Chile, 188, 189
Christoff, Kalina, 110
Clayton, Eli, 151
Climate Action Now (racing yacht),
  129–133
Climate Change and Sustainability
  Services, 69
Clipper Round the World yacht race,
  140, 152
Cognitive flexibility, 124
Cognitive reappraisal, 1–24, 190
  benefits of, 15
  changing perspectives with, 9–11
  effect of, on brain, 16–19
  personal story of, 3–9
  practice of, 19–21
  by salespeople, 11–16
  steps for building, 21–23
  of stories, 51
Cognitive reappraisal ability (CRA),
  18–19
Cognitive therapy, 39
Confidence, 33–40
Connected Commons, 175
Coping skills, 10–11
Core values, 95–99
Corporate environment:
  and innovation, 123

purpose in, 84–88
reframing in, 11
Cortisol, 149
CRA (cognitive reappraisal ability),
  18–19
Craig, Nick, 91–93
Crean, Tom, 187
"Creating a Growth Mindset"
  (Johnston), 63
Critical thinking, 125
Crossing the Swell (Gleeson and
  Holmes), 41, 47–48
Curiosity, 114

Dalai Lama, 23
Damon, Bill, 83
Daydreaming, 110–111, 125
Debebe, Gelaye, 97–98
Deloitte, 12
Depression, 18–19
Derler, Andrea, 60
Dominowski, Roger, 117
Dopamine, 89
Down Time, 174
Dreaming big, 108–116, 125–126
Duckworth, Angela, 31–32, 99
Dutton, Jane, 97–98
Dweck, Carol, 57, 64, 66, 73, 190

EA (Electronic Arts), 151–153
Education, focus on, 164–166
Effort:
  necessary in growth mindset, 67–74
  necessary to capitalize on
    opportunities, 58–59
  preparation as, 139–140
Effron, Mark, 179
EI (*see* Emotional intelligence)
8 Steps to High Performance (Effron),
  179
Electronic Arts (EA), 151–153
Elephant Island, 186–188
Emma (ship), 188

Emotional energy:
 building skills for, 152–153
 importance of balancing, 50
 for personal sustainability, 176–178
Emotional intelligence (EI):
 and innovation, 123
 and personal sustainability, 176
"Emotional Intelligence and
  Employee Creativity," 123
Emotional regulation, 16–17, 176–177
Emotions:
 labeling of, 177
 learning to recognize, 22–23
 and sleep, 179–180
Employee engagement:
 increasing, 70
 and job crafting, 99
 and purpose at work, 91
 at purpose-driven organizations,
  85–86
 and social connectedness, 175
Employees:
 as intrapreneurs, 118
 looking for companies with
  purpose, 69–70
The Endurance (ship), 186
Endurance Expedition, 185–189
Environmental activism, 82–83,
  96–97, 99–101
Environments, for innovation, 119–126
Ericsson, Anders, 174
Expressive writing, 22–23, 81
EY Beacon Institute, 86

Failures:
 and innovation, 116–119, 126
 as part of creative process, 118
Fake it till you make it, 33–40, 51
Falkland Islands, 188
Family, as social support, 144–146
Fear:
 dealing with, 4–5
 in face of health problems, 75–76

of failure, 64, 119
 and innovation, 118
 of the unknown, 59–60, 153
Feedback:
 honest, 61
 learning from, 60–63, 71–73
Fields, Amy, 179–180
Financial inclusion, 86–87
Finding one's purpose, 79–83, 89–102
Fisher, Jen, 179–180
fMRI (functional magnetic resonance
  imaging), 16
Focus Time, 174
Frankl, Viktor, 89, 102
"From Purpose to Impact" (Craig and
  Snook), 91
Fuller, Buckminster, 100–101
Functional magnetic resonance
  imaging (fMRI), 16

Geilan, Michelle, 148
George, J., 124
Gladwell, Malcom, 174
Glazer, Judith, 149
Glazer, Richard, 149
Gleeson, Paul, xiii, 27–33, 35–38,
  40–43, 47–52, 190
Glucocorticoids, 142
Goldberg, Dave, 142
Google, 112
Google X, 112
Gorsky, Alex, 88
Grace Hopper Celebration of Women
  in Computing, 66
Grant, Adam, 143
Greater good, contributions to, 99–102
Grit, 25–52, 190
 building perseverance, 46–50
 and passion, 40–46
 personal story of, 27–33
 psychological research on, 39
 and self-talk, 33–40
 steps for building, 50–51

Grit (Duckworth), 31, 99
Growth mindset, 53–76, 190
    beliefs about, 63–67
    learning from feedback, 60–63
    personal story of having, 55–58
    risk and effort necessary in, 67–72
    seeking opportunities, 58–60
    steps for building, 73–74
    in view of change, 112–113
    and views of failure, 117–118
Guimarães, R. M., 144

Habit(s):
    cognitive reappraisal as, 15–16, 23
    and innovation, 113–114
Happiness:
    as choice, 23–24
    meaningful purpose vs., 90
Hard work, 58–59
Harrington, Tony, 69
Harvard Business School, 86
Hawaii, 138
Health benefits, of purpose, 89–90
Hogan, Susan, 179–180
Holmes, Tori, xiii, 27–33, 35–38,
    40–43, 47–52, 190
Holocaust, 89
Honest feedback, 61
Hospital maintenance workers, 98–99
"How People Learn to Become
    Resilient" (Konnikova), 137–138
Hurst, Aaron, 90–91

If-then scenario plans, 142
Illness, facing, 74–76
Imperial Trans-Antarctic Expedition,
    xi–xii, 185–189
Imposter syndrome, 35–36, 38
Incubation, of ideas, 111–112
Indian Ocean, 100
Injuries:
    cognitive reappraisal in recovery
        from, 5–9

    growth mindset in facing, 75–76
    recovery from, xvii–xviii
Innovation, 103–126, 191
    dreaming big for, 108–116
    environments for, 119–125
    failures and, 116–119
    personal story of, 105–108
    steps for building, 125–126
Innovation Lab, 125
Intention, 42–43
Internal locus of control, 51
Intrapreneurs, employees as, 118
Invention, 109
It's Not About the Bike (Armstrong),
    41

Jacksonville Landing, Florida, 151
James Caird (rowboat), 187
Jetpacks, 115–116
Jetwing, 106, 116
Job:
    career, purpose, and, 85
    enhancing, with connections to core
        values, 97–99
Job crafting, 96–99
Johnston, Ian, 63
Journal of Cognitive Neuroscience, 16

Kahn, Louis, 122
Kauai, Hawaii, 138
King Haadon Bay, 187
Klawe, Maria, 66
Kleitman, Nathan, 174
Knox-Johnston, Robert, 140
Kodak, 114
Konnikova, Maria, 137–138

Landa, Tyge, 5
Leadership capabilities:
    and adventuring, x–xi, 70–71
    of Sir Ernest Shackleton, 188–189
Leadership development:
    and finding one's purpose, 101–102

with lessons from adventure world, 71

Learning, from feedback, 60–63

Lee, Shevaun, 11–12

Leveraging Grit for Leadership Success (Sudbrink), 39

LinkedIn, 91

Locus of control, 36–37, 51

Loehr, Jim, 171

Madden NFL (video game), 151

"Manage Your Energy, Not Your Time" (Schwartz and McCarthy), 176

Man's Search for Meaning (Frankl), 89

Maritime Rescue Coordination Centre in Cape Town, 135

Marques, Joan, 90

Mastercard, 86–87

Mathews, Mark, xii, 3–9, 13–14, 17–19, 22–24, 190

McCarthy, Catherine, 176

McFadyen, Matt, xiii, 55–56, 58–64, 67–76, 190

McGill University, 164–165

McKinsey Global Institute, 64–65

Meaning:
  benefits of having, 89
  and purpose, 84–85
  at work, 91

Mental energy:
  enhanced by physical activity, 178–179
  importance of balancing, 49–50
  for personal sustainability, 173–175

Messner, Reinhold, 187

Meyerson, Bernard, 112

Microsoft, 65–67

Millennials, 90, 91

Milward, Claude, 189

Mindfulness, 177–178

Mindset (Dweck), 57, 66

"Mindsets and Human Nature" (Dweck), 64

Montreal, Canada, 161–163

Moonshots, 112

Mount Everest, 107

Mountain climbing, 106–108, 115

Mowbray, Tony, 60–61, 73

Nadella, Anupama, 66

Nadella, Satya, 65–67

National Geographic magazine, 64

Nature, innovation and, 119–120

Negativity:
  following a negative event, 9–10
  and innovation, 124–125
  natural tendency toward, 36
  toward change, 113

Nemmani, Karthik, 31

The Neurochemistry of Positive Conversation (Richard and Judith Glazer), 149

NeuroLeadership Institute, 60, 119, 174

Neuroplasticity, 72

Nokia, 114

North Pole, 55–56

Northwest Passage crossing, 154–155

Obituaries, 80–81, 93

Ocean rowing, 27–33, 52, 95–97, 100–101

Ochsner, Kevin, 16

"Oh What Happiness! Finding Joy and Purpose Through Work" (Marques), 90

Oiselle, 44

Olympics, 172–173

O'Neill, Shane, 40

Openness, to new experiences, 124

Opportunities:
  saying no to, 169
  seeking, 58–60, 73

Option B (Sanberg and Grant), 143
Organizational climate, 123
"Organizational Support for
    Intrapreneurship and Its
    Interactions with Human
    Capital to Enhance Innovative
    Performance" (Alpkan), 118
Organizations, purpose-driven,
    85–86
Oxytocin, 89, 149

Pacific Ocean, 97
Parenthood, 33–34
Passion:
    and grit, 40–46
    growing spark into, 96–97
    questioning, 116–117
Pemberton, Rex, xiii, 105–110, 114–
    117, 119–120, 123–124, 191
Performance:
    adventure as litmus test for, xi–xiii
    and balance, 173
Perseverance, building, 46–51
Personal sustainability, 157–183
    balancing your energies for, 172–
        173, 180–182
    defining, 167–168
    emotional energy for, 176–178
    mental energy for, 173–175
    personal story of, 159–167
    physical energy for, 178–180
    relationship energy for, 175–176
    setting boundaries for, 169–170
    steps for building, 183
    and ultradian rhythms, 170–172
Perspectives, changing, 9–11
Peru, 82–83, 106–107
PFC (prefrontal cortex), 19
Philips, Eric, 64, 67–68, 73
Physical activity:
    and innovation, 122
    and mental performance, 178–179
    unintended benefits of, 48–49

Physical energy:
    importance of balancing, 50
    for personal sustainability, 178–180
PIL (purpose in life), 89–91
Pink, Daniel, 13
Play Time, 174
*PNAS (Proceedings of the National
    Academy of Sciences)*, 110
Polar exploration, 55–56, 67–71
Polio, 121
Posey, Amy, ix, 74–75
Positive mood, 123–124
The Power of Full Engagement (Loehr
    and Schwartz), 171
Practice, of cognitive reappraisal,
    19–22
Prefrontal cortex (PFC), 19
Preparation:
    cognitive reappraisal before
        negative events, 20
    and perseverance, 47–50
    and resilience, 139–140
    for worst-case scenarios, 141–142,
        152–153
PricewaterhouseCoopers (PwC),
    69–71
*Proceedings of the National Academy of
    Sciences* (PNAS), 110
Product-based focus, of sales
    profession, 12
"Promoting Insightful Problem
    Solving" (Ansburg and
    Dominowski), 117
Public speaking career, 68
Purpose, 77–102, 191
    benefits of finding, 89–91
    in corporate environment, 84–88
    employees looking for companies
        with, 69–70
    finding one's, 91–102
    personal story of finding one's,
        79–83
Purpose at Work study (LinkedIn), 91

The Purpose Economy (Hurst), 90
Purpose in life (PIL), 89–91
Purpose-driven organizations, 85–86
PwC (PricewaterhouseCoopers),
    69–71

Ratey, John, 178–179
Realistic optimism:
    and resilience, 147–152
    stories with, 153–154
Recovery time, 148–149
Reframing (*See also* Cognitive
    reappraisal)
    in business environment, 11
    of failures, 117
    as preparation, 14
Relationship energy:
    importance of balancing, 50
    for personal sustainability, 175–176
Relationships (*See also* Social
    connectedness)
    perseverance in, 49
    sustaining strong, 153
Resilience, 127–155, 191–192
    building, 136–144
    personal story of, 129–136
    and realistic optimism, 147–152
    and social connectedness, 144–147
    steps for building, 152–155
"Resilience Is About How You
    Recharge, Not About How You
    Endure" (Achor and Geilan), 148
Risk(s):
    necessary in growth mindset, 67–74
    of not trying, 136–137
    willingness to take, and emotional
        intelligence, 123
Robertson, Taylor, 151
Rock, David, 119, 174–175
Rodriguez, Diego, 117
Rothe, Eugenio M., 111
Rotter, Julian B., 36
Rowing the Atlantic (Savage), 82

Sailing, 58–63, 129–136, 140–141,
    145–147
Salesforce, 88
Salespeople, 11–16
Salk, Jonas, 121–122
Salk Institute of Biological Studies,
    121–122
Sandberg, Sheryl, 142–143
Savage, Roz, xii–xiii, 79–83, 92–97,
    100–101, 190–191
Schwartz, Tony, 171, 176
Self-confidence, 182
Self-exploration, 93–94, 143–144
Self-talk:
    and grit, 33–40
    and innovation, 113
    and resilience, 148
    and stories that we tell ourselves,
        33–40, 51
Seligman, Martin, 148
Setbacks:
    coping with, 10–11
    growth mindset in facing, 75
    resilience in handling, 136
Shackleton, Sir Ernest, xi–xii, 185–189
Siegel, Daniel, 174–175
Sisters project, 101
Skydiving, 105–106, 114–115
Sleep, 179–180
Smith, Jed, 6
Snook, Scott A., 91–93
Social connectedness:
    and grit, 37, 44–45
    and leadership development, 71
    performance improved by, 61
    in personal life, 175–176
    and resilience, 144–147
    sustaining, 153
    at work, 147, 175
Societal norms, following, 79–80
Solutions-based focus, of sales
    profession, 12
South Georgia Island, 186–188

South Pole, 159–167
Southern Ocean, 61–63, 129, 136,
    145, 147
The Southern Sky (ship), 188
Spark:
    aligning, with core values, 95–99
    finding your, 93–95
Spark (Ratey), 178–179
Stakeholders, serving all, 88
Steps for building:
    cognitive reappraisal, 21–23
    grit, 50–51
    growth mindset, 73–74
    innovation, 125–126
    personal sustainability, 183
    resilience, 152–155
Stigma, associated with failure, 117
Stories:
    with realistic optimism, 153–154
    and resilience, 148
    that we tell ourselves, 33–40, 51
Stress:
    and glucocorticoids, 142
    as part of creative process, 118
    recovery from, and resilience,
        148–149
    and resilience, 138–139
    and social connectedness, 144
Stromness, South Georgia Island, 187
Sudbrink, Laurie, 39
Sunshine Coast Daily, 140
SUPER*MEGA*BOSS, ix
Surfing, 3–9
Sutton, Bob, 117

Taproot Foundation, 90
Thoreau, Henry David, 192

To Sell Is Human (Pink), 13
Toohey, Shane, viii, xiii–xviii
Troy, Allison, 18
Two Hummock Island, xv

Ultradian rhythms, 170–172, 183
Uncertainty, 59–60
"Understanding When Bad Moods
    Foster Creativity and Good Ones
    Don't" (George and Zhou), 124

Valcour, Monique, 170
Vallely, Kevin, ix–x, xiii, 122, 154–
    155, 159–168, 180–182, 192
Values, core, 95–99
Venables, Stephen, 187
Video gaming industry, 150–152
Volkswagen Motors (VW), 87–88

Werner, Emmy, 138–139
Wilson, Andrew, 151
Wingsuit flying, 114–115
Winterkorn, Martin, 87–88
Worsley, Frank, 187
Worst-case scenarios, 141–142,
    152–153
Writing:
    expressive, 22–23, 81
    as reflection, 150
Wrzesniewski, Amy, 97–100

Yahoo!, 114
Yelcho (ship), 188
"You Snooze, You Win" (Fisher, et
    al.), 179–180

Zhou, J., 124

About the Authors

AMY POSEY translates the science of performance into practical work habits for global Fortune 500 companies. Sharing her lessons learned and making research relevant for the modern-day business leader, she helps people apply the latest science into how they can be better humans at work and beyond. As former CEO of The AIP Group and current founder and CEO of SUPER*MEGA*BOSS, Amy has spent the last 20 years uncovering practical ways people can work smarter. She has worked with companies including Apple, The Bill and Melinda Gates Foundation, Cisco, Deloitte, Google, HP, Mastercard, McKinsey, McKesson, Microsoft, Paypal, and VMware. Amy earned her executive masters with distinction in Applied Neuroscience and Leadership from the Neuroleadership Institute. She also earned her MBA with honors from DePaul University's campus in the Kingdom of Bahrain, where she lived and worked for two years broadening her global perspective. She has a BA in English, Education, and Writing with distinction from Purdue University. An adventurer at heart, she has explored more than 60 countries on all seven continents, most recently as part of an 11-person expedition to the Arctic with her coauthor, crossing Baffin Island, Nunavut, Canada, on foot in winter.